NORTHERN SURREY

Edited by Allison Dowse

First published in Great Britain in 2003 by
YOUNG WRITERS
Remus House,
Coltsfoot Drive,
Peterborough, PE2 9JX
Telephone (01733) 890066

SB ISBN 1 84460 273 7

FOREWORD

Young Writers was established in 1991 as a foundation for promoting the reading and writing of poetry amongst children and young adults. Today it continues this quest and proceeds to nurture and guide the writing talents of today's youth.

From this year's competition Young Writers is proud to present a showcase of the best poetic talent from across the UK. Each hand-picked poem has been carefully chosen from over 66,000 'Hullabaloo!' entries to be published in this, our eleventh primary school series.

This year in particular we have been wholeheartedly impressed with the quality of entries received. The thought, effort, imagination and hard work put into each poem impressed us all and once again the task of editing was a difficult but enjoyable experience.

We hope you are as pleased as we are with the final selection and that you and your family will continue to be entertained with *Hullabaloo! Northern Surrey* for many years to come.

CONTENTS

Olivia Edwardson (11) 1

Ambleside Junior School
Asha Laroy (11) 1
Kajal Bhagwandas (10) 2
Naimah Choudhury 2
Simon Coomes (10) 3
Rebecca Keen (10) 4
Danielle Best (10) 5
Candice Phillips (11) 6
Sarah Fancy (11) 7
David Walsh (10) 8

Blackdown Primary School
Stephanie Allen (11) 9
Katie McMonagle (10) 10
Perry Bloss (10) 10
TJ Archibald (10) 11
Joe Robinson (10) 11
Yasmin Phair (10) 12
Rhys Harrison (11) 12

Downside Lodge School
Jack D'souza Toulson (9) 13
Aaron Bowers (9) 13
Reece Foster (8) 14
Ivie Aderibigbe (9) 14
Johan Reker (9) 15
Kunihiko Nishimura (10) 16
Holly Worthington (10) 17
Ellie Rose (10) 18
Payal Chand (10) 18
Amy Winter (10) 19
George Neale (9) 19
Yuria Inanaga (10) 20
Albert Aka (9) 20

Daniel Collins (10) 21
Lewis Phenix (9) 21

Halstead Prep School
Jessica Heath (10) 22
Megan Whitehead (10) 23
Janey Hurran (10) 24
Victoria Deyong-Burgess (9) 25
Olivia Fox (9) 26
Natalie Barber (9) 27
Brooke Theis (9) 28
Cassandra Mason (10) 29
Becky Lane (9) 30
Chloe Birch (10) 31
Elizabeth Kelly (10) 32
Rosanna Knottenbelt (9) 33
Amy Lance (10) 34
Katy Warham (10) 35
Kirstin Cooper (10) 36
Sophie Fowler-Tutt (9) 37
Ellen Elphick (9) 38
Elizabeth Gardner (10) 39
Amy Bowerin (9) 40
Abigail Binns (9) 41
Amy Piercy (9) 42
Elly Sams (9) 43
Sarah-Jayne K Stamper (9) 44

Horsell CE Primary School
Sam May (10) 44
Jessica Burrowes (11) 45
Christopher Purvis (10) 46
Michele Rice (11) 46
Curtis Hylton (10) 47
Robert Prince (10) 47
Alice Spencer (11) 48
Laura Bradbury (10) 49
William Sadler (10) 49

Mark Foster (11) 50
Kian Henry (11) 50
David Oliver (10) 51
Charis Rokins (11) 51
Connor Hargreaves (10) 52
Katy Rhodes (10) 52
James Farrier (10) 53
Anna Westgate (10) 54
Gemma Cook (10) 55
Kimberley Reygadas (11) 56
Evan Bowen (10) 56
Emma Rawlings (11) 57
Scott Maher (10) 58
Louise Sellars (10) 59
Matthew Goodey (10) 60
Shona Probert (11) 61
Jack Coffey (10) 62
Rebecca Challis (10) 63
Sam Smith (10) 64
Alice Cross (10) 64
Jamie Squelch (10) 65
Richard Hylton (10) 66
Chris Wallis (11) 66
Morgan Rimay-Muranyi (10) 67
Henna Ahmed (11) 68
Susannah Schrock (10) 69
Lawrence Barrott (11) 70

Mytchett Primary School

Aaron McDonald (9) 70
Charlotte Crabb (11) 71
Harriet Cooper (10) 72
Lindsey Parker (10) 73
Sofie Kent (10) 74
Bobbie Owen (11) 74
Sarah Byrnes (11) 75
Daniel Balmbra (10) 75
Kathryn Roke (9) 76

Michael Newland (11) 76
Melissa Plom (10) 77
Jake White (11) 78
Ryan Howson (9) 79
Ryan Wells (10) 79
Laura Hylands (9) 80
Abbi Field (9) 81
Daniel Hardman (10) 82
Natasha Ward (10) 83
Zoë Filshie (9) 84
James Hagan (9) 85
Alexander Barlow (10) 85
Bromwyn Brett (9) 86
Marc Simmonds (9) 87
Katie Patterson (9) 88
Nicola Gallop (10) 89
Charlotte Lindley (10) 89
Josh Kipping (10) 90
Dominique Quinlan (9) 91
Rebecca Holford (10) 92
Srijit Venkat (10) 93

New Monument Primary School
Jacque Bayliss (8) 93
Shamile Chaudhry (11) 94
Sara Munir (11) 95
Mohammed Ali (11) 96
Tapiwa Moyo (11) 97
Rubina Miah (11) 98
Paul Nadeem (10) 99

Purley Oaks Primary School
Holly Clarke (9) 99
Harriet Fiddimore (8) 100
Krassi Petrova (9) 101
Ben Elliott (8) 101
Nathan Shaw (9) 102
Jordan Giddings (9) 103

Kiri Moon (8) 104
Rebecca Harvey (9) 104
Jessica Elsey (9) 105
Kaitlyn Sheeran (8) 106
Rebecca David (10) 106
Tahnée Seagrave (7) 107
Darcie Kelly (8) 107
Joanne Matheson (8) 108
Lola Meredith (8) 108
Marsha Egwea (11) 109
Natasha McInerney (11) 109
Fiona Dougan (11) 110
Holly Burraway Andrews (11) 111
Sharn Brown (10) 111
Olivia Procter (11) 112
Dyane Baden-Moore (11) 112
Danielle Sheeran (10) 113
Luis Shove (10) 113
Hannah Clarke (10) 114
Emily Brown (11) 114
Philippa Mensah (10) 115
Scott Friel (11) 115
Daisy Milward (10) 115
Aisha Haughton (10) 116
Bobby Walker (11) 116
Vicky Gunner (10) 117
Ben Burke & Chevoy Johnson (9) 117
Katie Elliott (10) 118
Conor Hack (11) 119
Eve Livesley (10) 119
Emma Grogan (10) 120
Shivam Patel (9) & Bradley Talbot (10) 120

Reedham Park School

Arjoon Niranjan (9) 121
Manu Babu (9) 122
Aaron McGuigan (9) 122
Hayley Bogaerts (9) 123

Nasha Raman (11) 124
Imogen Wainwright-Jones (9) 125
Faye Kearns (10) 126
Lucy Mackenzie (10) 127
Marina Guy (11) 127
Oliver Ash (10) 128
Toni Akinajo (9) 128
Temilade Oni (10) 129
Jessica Sneddon (10) 129
Joanna Parkins (9) 130
Sonya Sivadasan (11) 130
Stephanie Lawden (10) 131
Joel Schoburgh-Crooks (9) 131
Andrew Guest (8) 132
Annabelle Ade-Jones (9) 132
Vicki Laffey (10) 133
Georgia Price (10) 134
Clara-Louis McKrieth (8) 135
Rhia Sharma (11) 136
Jessica Russell (11) 137
Lucy Doyle (10) 138
Abi McGilvray (10) 139
Ellie Prior (9) 140
Tharini Thirukkumar (9) 141
Andrew Russell (9) 142
Stephen Dowset (10) 143
Ashleigh Hall (9) 144
James Hedges (10) 145
Ashleigh Blackwood (8) 146
Berenice Graham (8) 147
Marissa Beatty (8) 148
Jade Sherwill (8) 149
Marissa Nurse (8) 150
Selexis Stephens (10) 151
Bronte Jack (8) 152

Royal Kent CE Primary School

Yousif Mahdi (10) 152
William Janes (10) 153
Otis Brayer (9) 153
Katherine Yearley (10) 154
Bethany Bradford (10) 154
Rhys Davies (10) 155
Noah Granger (9) 155
Rowena Hill (10) 156
Emily Smith-Drane (10) 157
Amy Stewart (9) 158
Victoria Millward (9) 159
Chantelle Sayers (10) 160
Elizabeth Springford (9) 161
Jonathan Berry (10) 162
Marcos Zakakiotis 162
Gemma Skilton (9) 163
Ben Thomas (10) 163
Eleanor Hutchings (9) 164
Eleanor Singer (9) 165

St David's School, Purley

Emily Bacon (10) 165
Ryan Reid (10) 166
Joseph Rifaat (10) 166
Matthew Watson (9) 167
Olivia Rogers (9) 167
Becky Smith (11) 168
Jay Patel (10) 168
Rachael Sanders (11) 169
Adam Bowley (10) 169
Olayinka Lauson (11) 170
Sarah Dixon (11) 171
Annabel Rathbone (9) 171
Daniel Ashby (10) 172
Thomas Tawse (9) 172
Nuala Armstrong-Walsh (9) 173
Abigail Wilson (10) 173

Rhiannon Cogbill (9) 174

St Martin's CE Junior School, Epsom
Katie Staines (9) 174
Madeleine Cole (11) 175
Gemma Drewitt (11) 175
Fiona Middleton (9) 176
Amani Salam (8) 176
Hannah Foxley (9) 177
Jessica Chinchen (8) 177
Nicola Boult (10) 178
Eluned Broom (10) 179
Jeremy Hunt (7) 180
Katie Sevenoaks (10) 181
Tessa Derry (9) 181
Christopher Duncan (10) 182
Emma Woolgar (9) 183
Jodie Rogers (8) 184
Emily Ranson (9) 185
Rebecca Green (9) 186
Emma Brooker (10) 186
Holly Soodhoo (10) 187
Keshini Jayawardana (9) 187
Andrew Taylor (9) 188

Sanderstead Junior School
Sonal Patel (11) 188
Darren Emmanuel (10) 189
Anay Patel (9) 189
Haruka Mukai (11) 189
Isidahome Aligbe (10) 190
Ayumah Asigri (11) 190
Siân Williams (9) 191
Shin Nakamae (10) 191
Alice Warrington (11) 192
Natsuko Mukai (9) 192
Mariko Tanaka (10) 193
Liam Sanders (9) 193

Stamford Green Primary School
Natalie Cummins (9) 194
Christina Low (8) 194
Catherine Walsh (9) 195
Alex Willcocks (8) 195
Imogen Corbett (11) 196
Amy McCormack (8) 196
Emily Breese (8) 197
Eleanor Williams (8) 197

TASIS The American School In England
Griffin Leeds (10) 197
Mary Buswell (10) 198
Kathleen Jump (11) 199
Philippe O'Connor (10) 200
Katerina Kaczmarski (11) 201
Charlotte Cushing (9) 201
Thurston Smalley (10) 202
Katlin Bole (10) 202
Emily Goode (10) 203
Karina Zetterberg (11) 203
Emily Churchill (9) 204
Camila Aguais (10) 204
Parker Malone (10) 205
Meredith Weber (10) 206

The Dawnay School
James Wheeler (8) 206
Cat Romer (10) 207
Lily Hankin (10) 207
Gail Commandeur (11) 208
Luke Rance (9) 208
Amy Parr (8) 209
Luke Culley (8) 209
Robert Gray (8) 210
Harley Buck (10) 210
Max Denton (8) 211
Gareth Keen (8) 211

Alice Mennell (8)	212
Claire Cursley (11)	212
Nathan Farrell (10)	213
Sarah El-Baghdady (11)	213
Sammy Iftikhar (10)	214
Fraser Aberdeen (9)	214
Anusha Young (9)	215
Kerrina Gray (10)	215
Rebecca Jones (8)	216
Amanda Apps (10)	216
Daniel Leach (10)	217
Julia Smith (9)	217
Jessica Leitch (10)	218
Sophie Clowser (10)	218
Jack Denton (10)	219
Anthony Bligh (10)	220
Cherry Cattermole (10)	220
Laura Cronin (9)	221
Emma Houslander (9)	222
Mariam El-Baghdady (8)	222
Rebecca Lambert (9)	223
Alex Rollins (9)	223
Catherine Ryder (10)	224
Chloe Walker-Trivett (9)	224
Natalie Goodacre (9)	225
Toby Irwin (10)	226
Daniel Morrison (10)	226
David Andrews (9)	227
Ben Fisher (8)	227
Ed Anstis (10)	228
Anita Massimo (9)	228
Robert Cunnett (10)	229
Ella Smith (9)	229
James Woodley (10)	230
Ross Elliott (9)	230
Juliet Grenville (9)	231
Charlotte Black (8)	231
Josh Rapley (9)	232

Madeleine Halls (8) 232
Harriet Connor (10) 233
Stephanie Law (9) 233
Elizabeth Childes (9) 234
William Learmont (8) 234
Ben Bedford (10) 235
Maria Tilt (10) 235
Jenny Pemberton (10) 236
Iona Doig (8) 236
Rachel Cumper (9) 237
Rianne Elliott (8) 237
Rebecca Dawson (9) 238
George Chard (8) 238
Joanna Russell (8) 239
Samuel Hudson (8) 239
Alexandra Sarah Hastie (8) 240
Lewis Andrews (10) 240
Thomas Dicks (10) 241
Charlotte Bateman (11) 241
Jade Leach (11) 242
Elizabeth Pymm (11) 242
Lucy Hunt (8) 243
Katherine Hughes (9) 243
Rose Williams (8) 244
Michael Black (9) 244
Emma Paige (9) 245
Cameron Fox (10) 245
Rebecca Coles (10) 246
Beth Woodham (10) 246
Kristian Eaton (9) 246

Woodside Junior School
Janet Foskett (9) 247
Charlie Penfold (8) 247
Ross Marshall (8) 248
Ellie Burtenshaw (9) 248
Sian Fitzpatrick (9) 249
Thomas Bean (10) 249

Priyel Upadhyaya (8)	250
Tom Barry (10)	250
Geoffrey Whitby (8)	251
Teri Bailey (10)	251
Naomi Harrison (9)	252
Mariam Farooqui (10)	252
Christopher Newlyn (9)	253
Cristie Jarvis (10)	253
Georgina Amor (8)	254
Leanne Walker (9)	254
Harry Wall (9)	255
Ashley Sullivan (10)	255
Asif Ali (8)	256
Ross Goodey (10)	256
Samantha Porter (8)	257
Hannah Rossi (9)	257
Holly Sud (9)	258
Ben Lawson (10)	258
Alexandra Kelland (9)	259
Nikisha Cantle (10)	259
James Giddy (9)	260
George Davis (9)	260
Kalifa Best (9)	261
Emily Mills (9)	261
David Parke (9)	262
James Hatfield (9)	263
Aaron Keefe (9)	264
Daniel Turner (9)	265
Lewis Slane (9)	266
Lewis Hill (9)	266
Coral Jardine (9)	266
Jordan Long (9)	267
Dean Leggatt (9)	267
Charlie McCormick (8)	268
Lindsey Gwilliam (9)	268
Joe Couzens (9)	269
Jamie Mills (9)	269
Melissa Theedom (9)	270

Rebecca Vernon (10) 270
Keith Wheeler (9) 271
Bethany Scott (10) 271
Paris Hanson (9) 272
Harry Forrester (9) 272
Charlotte Cross (10) 273
Ashley Monckton (9) 273
Rianna Matthews (10) 274
Christopher Stobbs (10) 274
Daniel O'Connor (10) 275
Frances Thompson (10) 275

The Poems

THE MAGIC BOX

(Based on 'Magic Box' by Kit Wright)

I will put in the box . . .
The tiniest fairy's wand,
The contract that was shown to determine peace,
One silk, scarlet scarf.

I will put in the box . . .
The first beautiful leaf that fell in autumn,
The love and care of my mum.

I will put in the box . . .
My true feelings,
My inner strength,
The football that won the World Cup,
The silk red rose on my grandad's grave.

My box will have the finest silver,
Shimmering diamonds on top,
And inside will be the invisible love
God gave me.

Olivia Edwardson (11)

ANGELS WHAT ARE THEY?

'What are angels like?' I would say every night
Are they in Heaven, in the light?
Sitting in the hands of God.
Angels listening to the plans of God.
Their sweet little faces glowing with might.
See them sitting on clouds of light.

Asha Laroy (11)
Ambleside Junior School

My Three Friends

I have three friends who are really cool.
They play with me in the swimming pool.

They dress really really smart.
They have very kind heart.

They are my best friends.
But sometimes they drive me round the bend.

They're as gentle as a feather
We like hanging out together.

We have lots of games to play
We have lots of things to say.

Kajal Bhagwandas (10)
Ambleside Junior School

The Dark

As I lay in the dark in the dead of the night,
I crept out of bed, shaking with fright,
I crept around the house,
Creeping crawling as quiet as a mouse,
It was then I heard the bone-shivering *bang!*
Following after it, a terrifying clang!
I crept downstairs to the source of the racket,
It was coming from outside, I grabbed my jacket,
Then as I turned to the source of the din,
I realised that it was none other than a cat in the bin!

Naimah Choudhury
Ambleside Junior School

SLUGS

Slugs, slugs
Crawl through doors
Over the grass
And under the floors

Slugs, slugs
Are like snails
They both leave
Silvery trails

Slugs, slugs
Are so slow
They take such
A time to go

Slugs, slugs
Are a pest
They are not
A welcome guest

Slugs, slugs
Eat a good meal
From the fruit
And veg they steal

Slugs, slugs
Love the rain
Like to be near
A dirty drain

Slugs, slugs
Are a feast
To all manner
Of bird and beast.

Simon Coomes (10)
Ambleside Junior School

ALONE

I'm in the house alone
I'm alone, alone
The lights turn off
I'm alone, alone
I hear a crash
I'm alone, alone
I creep downstairs
I'm alone, alone
I see a tall figure walk down the hall
I'm alone, alone
I follow the figure
I'm alone, alone
My heart is thumping really fast
I'm alone, alone
The rain begins to fall
I'm alone, alone
I see the figure has something sharp in its hand
I'm alone, alone
I trip! Did it hear me?
I'm alone, alone
It carries on walking
I'm alone, alone
It walks down deep to the basement, I follow
My teeth began to chatter
The figure turns! I'm trapped . . .

Rebecca Keen (10)
Ambleside Junior School

JUST RIGHT

I was hopping to the shop to buy me a pet
Because I had never had my own pet yet.
When I got there I opened up the door
Frogs, hogs, dogs and more.

I went over to the rabbit hutch to see what was there
There were two big rabbits and one small hare
I picked one up, so cuddly they were,
But then I remembered I was allergic to fur.

I put down the rabbit and let out a sneeze
I looked at the fish caught from the deepest seas.
Then I remembered you eat fish with a fork
Besides I prefer animals that I can walk.

I went over the guinea pig
I didn't believe it, he was as skinny as a twig.
I'm not having him, he wouldn't last a day
He was nowhere close to OK.

Maybe a parrot would fit my suit
But when I got there he let out a hoot.
He's too loud, he would keep me up all night,
Will I ever get a pet that's just right?

I want an animal, maybe a bat
But they fly around the room so that blows that.
I've seen all the animals in the shop
I don't like animals that slither or hop.

I don't like rabbits or even dogs,
I don't like guinea pigs, cats or frogs.
Will I have a pet or will I not?
I'm too picky, I fuss alot.

I came to the conclusion I don't want a pet
It's upsetting I know, but I'm not ready, at least not yet.

Danielle Best (10)
Ambleside Junior School

First Day

On my very first day
Our friendly head
showed me around and said,

'Candice you'll be happy here
There's loads of books and a library there.'

Miss Lauder made me feel quite at home
The playgrounds and corridors looked exciting to roam.
Ambleside it sounds so good
Most of all the building is made out of wood.
And then out of the corner of my eye
I saw a man with a huge tie.

'Mr Weigman is my name
and maths is my game.
Candice, what's 9 x 8?'
I stood, I froze, I thought it got late.

No matter how hard I tried
I could not think of the answer even if I had lied.

It's now five months later and still I feel great
Ambleside, my second home, I'll never be late!

Candice Phillips (11)
Ambleside Junior School

A Poem About Sweets

I like chocolate
I like sweets
I hate truffles
I love treats!

Sweets are yummy
Sweets are great
I hate to share them
With my mates!

Caramel, fudge
Cookies, cream
All the flavours
In my dreams!

These are the best
Really scrum
But my mum usually buys them
For my tum!

Lollipops, bubblegum,
Gobstoppers too,
Especially bubblegum
Which I have to chew!

These are yum
And the best,
My favourite is caramel
But I still love the rest!
Mmmmm!

Sarah Fancy (11)
Ambleside Junior School

Animal Poems

There was a horse
who was three,
he jumped the fence
and broke his knee.

There was a camel
who was four
he sat on a chair
whilst shutting the door.

There was a bee
who was five
he saw a cat
in a beehive.

There was a giraffe
who was six
he knew how to
pick up sticks.

There was a monkey
who was seven
he went on a train
all the way to Devon.

There was a frog
who was eight
he met a policeman
on a date.

There was a dog
who was nine
he hung his collar
on the line.
There was a fish
who was ten,
he went to London
to see Big Ben.

David Walsh (10)
Ambleside Junior School

My Harry Potter Hole

My room is like my home inside my house.
I love Harry Potter, so I call it my Harry hole.
It is plastered with pictures of, you guessed it,
Harry Potter!
I keep a special bin with any pictures of the cut outs
of the characters from the books.
I have an LG video recorder, a TV, a desk, and a
huge wardrobe inside my room.
I think I spend most of my time in there
because it is my own space.
Every time I'm in there I'll watch a video
or normal telly or read.
It is a tip but I love it!

Stephanie Allen (11)
Blackdown Primary School

My Little Brother

My brother is so small,
My mum said he'll grow really tall.
I just laugh and walk away,
It's hard to think of it anyway.
Mum says that because she can't wait,
Till he grows up and makes a mate.
I can't wait for him to grow up,
So he can reach his own cup.
He always gets his own way,
Like he chooses the best treat of the day.

Katie McMonagle (10)
Blackdown Primary School

World War II

Peace for the last second
Then *bang*.
Innocent souls die.
Gunshots going up
Then nothing but silence.
The war's beginning
Gunshots flying in the air.
More souls gone.
Aeroplanes soaring the air.
Ambush . . . a trap
They shout,
'Run, run, run!'

Perry Bloss (10)
Blackdown Primary School

THE ICE CREAM SUNDAE

Cherry
On top
Strawberry
Sauce
Chocolate-
Flavoured
Ice cream
Hot fudge
M&Ms on top
Cooling taste
Creamy dessert
Sauce left at
The bottom
Smooth feel
On your
Tongue.

TJ Archibald (10)
Blackdown Primary School

THE WAR

War is scary, big loud noises,
The war is scary, very, very dangerous.
The war is scary, people get killed,
The war is scary, you have to leave your parents,
The war is scary, big bombs drop,
The war is scary, good job it hasn't happened to me.

Joe Robinson (10)
Blackdown Primary School

In The Waiting Room

We are waiting for the new baby to be born,
But I'm not too sure now, if I want a new baby
In the house.
Because it will . . . scream, bawl
Squeak all night or,
We might have a good and quiet baby.
We will find out soon,
As we are waiting in the waiting room.

Yasmin Phair (10)
Blackdown Primary School

The Black Hole

When I dream about me in a black hole,
I think I'm actually there.
I see strange things crawling in my hair.
I lose my heart, my wishes and my soul.
I have no home in this black hole.
I'd rather be somewhere else than here
But I can't get out until someone rescues me.
Then I'll be in my home,
Out of this hole.
Someone must save me.

Rhys Harrison (11)
Blackdown Primary School

WHISKERS

Oh Whiskers
Enjoy the summer
Chasing all the specks of dust
Enjoy the blazing sun
Beaming in the garden
Enjoy playing in the sun
With your brother
Enjoy the warm welcoming summer around you
Don't forget to watch out for the road
Then cross with us
And enjoy the long grass
On the Downs
Don't go hiding
Because I will go looking for you
And you will jump on my back from the nearest tree.

Jack D'souza Toulson (9)
Downside Lodge School

NEW WORDS

New words, new words,
Cosmic and corrode.
Armageddon and armadillo
Every day we learn new words.

What does Tyro mean?
What does Stanchion mean?
Life is complicated enough,
Without new words!

Aaron Bowers (9)
Downside Lodge School

HUGE MOON

I see in the sky a huge moon
and the stars glittering
and the moon shining
what a sight.
Ohh! Look there's a shooting star
and there's an aeroplane.
Or is it stars?
No it's an aeroplane
but you can see the moon most of all
shining as bright as the sun.

Reece Foster (8)
Downside Lodge School

THE CORNFIELD

The cornfield
Is a lovely place.
I visit it every weekend.
I love it so much.
It is wonderful!
Let me describe it to you.
It is like a lovely golden blanket
That will warm you instantly.
The corn is so soft
Which means the bread we make
Tastes lovely.
I love it!

Ivie Aderibigbe (9)
Downside Lodge School

The Football Game

At 3 o'clock it starts
The crowd are waving several parts.
Kick it, bash it,
Head it, smash it.
The away team are having fun
But at home they're number one.
The striker finds a hole
But still there is no goal.
They've had several shots,
And should have had the lot.
Eighty minutes gone
The manager brings the subs on
Into the last minute
Players taking the limit.
Ouch! That was hard
'You're sent off!' - red card
Penalty taken by Hill,
The crowd are wild and
It's one-nil.

Johan Reker (9)
Downside Lodge School

STAR

Now! And when I look at the clear sky,
I see stars like bright dust everywhere.
When I look into my planisphere,
Each group of stars has got a name.
Orion, Ursa Major, Pole Star, Caris Minor,
And they are in the sky.
'Soup's on!' my mum yelled.
Oh no it's already meal time! I thought.
After a three hour meal,
With my planisphere and torch,
I went to see the stars . . .
Wow! The stars have moved!
The star soldiers walking by,
'Lead in!' Orion shouted.
Everyone heard the voice and marched.
But . . . the Pole Star wasn't listening.
But it is good news to the people,
They'll know where the North is.
But Orion didn't care.

Kunihiko Nishimura (10)
Downside Lodge School

My Invisible Friend

My friend
called Katy
is very special
because nobody else can see her,
apart from me!

You see she is invisible,
it's great fun
to play with her.

My mum
my dad
my brother
they all think,
I'm mad!

They think
I talk to myself
but you see that's where they're wrong,
I talk to my friend Katy,
she's just invisible.

Holly Worthington (10)
Downside Lodge School

MINNIE

Minnie's my hamster
She acts very strange
Never goes in her wheel
And always escapes!
You never know where she'll run next
Under the washing machine
Behind the freezer
You just don't know.

Some days she'll sleep all day
Some days she goes frantic
You just never know with Minnie
Some days she will bite you
Some days she'll snuggle up in your arms
You really can't tell what will happen.

. . . But I love her.

Ellie Rose (10)
Downside Lodge School

MY HOME

My house is where I live
Where I play and study
It's made of bricks and sand
But my home is made up of my family.
My mum who is really loving
My dad who takes my side when I am wrong
And my brother,
Well he fights with me a lot.
My dog Timi who is really cute
This is my home.

Payal Chand (10)
Downside Lodge School

A Cat's Thought

Claws in my chair
I won't go away
This is my chair
And I'm here to stay.

Feet off my mat!
This is my home
This is where I sleep
All day long.

Hands off my bed
This is my room
This is where I sit
And groom all day.

Amy Winter (10)
Downside Lodge School

The Football Match

Chelsea are the team
So watch out for our evil scheme
You'll get a bruise
Or your team will lose
Ouch that was hard
Thierry Henry, red card!
Zola scores
The crowd applauds
Chelsea 1, Arsenal nil
What great skill.
Arsenal lose, Chelsea win,
Looks like Arsenal are in the sin bin!

George Neale (9)
Downside Lodge School

SPRINGTIME

Spring is a happy season
All the flowers bloom
And everyone is happy
The bees are busy too.

The beautiful butterflies
Fly across the sky
Blue, red and purple,
All over the world.

The baby foxes
All come out of their holes
And with their mothers' permission
They all come out to play.

And we, little children
Love this very season
For girls love pretty flowers
And the days are longer for boys.

Yuria Inanaga (10)
Downside Lodge School

THE SUN

The sun reminds me of a golf ball
The sun also reminds me of a beach ball
Every drop of sweat resembles the sun.

The sun is like an oven
The sun is like a planet
The sun looks like bits of fire put together.

Albert Aka (9)
Downside Lodge School

My Birthday

When the day is here
I jump up out of bed
And I run down the stairs to see what I've got.
Maybe it's a dog or maybe it's a TV
But whatever it is, I will be grateful.
But I still hope it's good
So when I rip open the paper
I find out what it is,
And then I go back to bed.

Daniel Collins (10)
Downside Lodge School

School

School, school
I love school
My favourite lesson
Is maths.
Even though
I love English.
I like to bite my pencil
And I love to lick my pen.
But all these I don't love as much
As . . .
School!

Lewis Phenix (9)
Downside Lodge School

TWINKLE AND SHIMMER OF SILVER SPARKLE

Twinkle and shimmer of silver sparkle
This is the night of wonder
The stars glow like beautiful fireflies gliding through the sky
The sky is dark ebony painted around the world
The trees whisper and jump out! All around me.
The moon like a bright lantern shines down on my face
I gaze at the pond as it twinkles and shines in the moon's gleam
And looks like a silver carpet
As I gaze something catches my eye
A spark of silver shimmering in the moonlight
Like a big deep colourful opal
I look again to see a magnificent *unicorn!*
Its mane of pure white cotton bouncing and waving in the breeze
Its eyes of diamonds twinkling
They stare unblinking
Its body of velvet, gleams with glittery stars
Its hooves of beaming black and white marble
With a horn that twizzles like an ice cream twister.

I blink, he is gone
My eyes search to find him
An empty surrounding
It was too good to be true
A tear comes to my eye
One more second to gaze upon his splendour
Would be worth the whole night

Twinkle and silver sparkle this is the night of wonder.

Jessica Heath (10)
Halstead Prep School

NOT ANY MORE ON THIS BEACH

This place that no longer is bustling with people,
Where children splashed in gentle waves
But not any more do you see sandcastles and people lying under
coloured brollies.
Not any more do you see children playing with beach balls.
Ice cream stalls and donkey rides, not any more . . . on this beach.
No more do children run around playing in the heaps of sand.
No more do people lie in the sun.

This beach was deserted with me,
I used to carry children on my back along the sunny shores.
Until one day I was led out as usual,
But that day I walked alone along the crisp cold shore.
Even the master deserted me,
Left me here alone to watch the waves,
To sit in the chill of a winter's day.

And as I walk along the shore day after day,
I feel as if a child is sitting on my back.
I see shadows of misty figures running around and playing,
But when I see the figures and feel the weight upon my back,
I shut my eyes and look again.
But there is nothing . . .
Only a cold crisp beach and chilling waves lapping the shore.

Megan Whitehead (10)
Halstead Prep School

My Dream Unicorn!

At midnight, the beautiful silver river flows
As the stars shine like dazzling pearls
Then suddenly out from the mist came
A crystal-coloured creature.

It was a shining silver horse
With a twisted horn
Which was like silver rock
The creature was then swishing its tail
While galloping through the lush green grassy fields.

My soft, cold shaking hand was held out
To the graceful, gorgeous unicorn
It stopped and gave a little rear in the air
As it showed off its stunning hooves.

It landed on the emerald-green grass again
And as it trotted over to me
Its tail twirled in the moonlight
It then knelt on its little thin legs
And flicked its attractive twisted tail
Onto its back.

It then stretched out its grey-silver wings
And we were off into the night sky,
With the dazzling stars close enough to touch
We flew past the silver moon,
Past the comets
And past the stars!

Then just as the sun was rising
We flew back down noiselessly
The unicorn knelt down
I leapt off
Then when I turned round it was gone!

Janey Hurran (10)
Halstead Prep School

THE UNICORN

A pebbled beach,
The sun so warm on my face,
The breeze ruffling my hair.
As I looked into the dancing waves
A beautiful creature
Came swimming towards me.
It was bright white
Its golden horn was elegantly twisted,
Its long white flowing tail,
Was in a silky plait,
Ribbons and little bells had been plaited
Into the unicorn's silky tail and mane,
The bells jingled merrily,
And seemed to say, 'Follow.'
So I ran and jumped onto the unicorn's
Abnormally warm back,
His coat was as soft as a chick's feathers,
He climbed the pebbles and then,
We were soaring,
Up, up into the cool air.
We passed clouds in very pretty shapes
A smoky grey cat stared at us as we passed,
We came to a bridge leading us,
Over a great shimmering lake,
The bridge was the rainbow,
I gave a little *whoop* of happiness,
I could see no one so I got off the unicorn's
Warm soft back,
As soon as I did he disappeared,
When I opened my eyes
I was in my warm soft bed.

Victoria Deyong-Burgess (9)
Halstead Prep School

THE BELIEF UNICORN

'Do you believe?' said the teacher expectantly
I did not believe in a magic unicorn
How could anyone believe in fairy tales?

Out at play, no one talked to me
I was left alone,
Thinking about the unicorn
The bell rang
I wandered in but I was stopped in my tracks.

The unicorn came out of the book
and tossed its magnificent mane angrily
I walked towards it, astonished by its beautiful presence
Its grey-white body was like . . .
a white linen tablecloth
draped over a large bony body
Its horn taken from a twisted marshmallow on a skewer
Its hooves like a small rippling river.

As I walked towards it, it swayed like a diver and
whispered,
'Believe in me!'
and faded and disappeared.
I believed.

Olivia Fox (9)
Halstead Prep School

ABROAD THOUGHTS FROM HOME

I swished through the waves,
Stones crackled under my feet
I swam and swam out from the golden shore,
My cousins by my side.
I came to a sudden halt,
Like a train coming to an emergency stop.
I spun around like a teacup at the fair,
Realising that my cousins had left me.
I felt uneasy,
Left on my own.
I swam through the rough waves,
Desperately searching for safety,
I heard seagulls flying above my head,
The water surrounding me was as cold as ice,
I swam a little further,
By now I was tired,
My feet ached and my eyes closing,
I looked up,
The sun was blazing in my eyes.
There before me was a grey blur,
It was a huge rock!
Exhausted I scrambled onto it,
My weary limbs limp
I was safe at last.

Natalie Barber (9)
Halstead Prep School

The Way Through The Woods

(A third verse for Rudyard Kipling's poem)

And as you enter the woods
On a deep winter's night,
The frost sinks its teeth
Into the cold, icy grass,
Three white ghosts appear . . .
What could they want?
I notice they are standing
In the middle of the old lost road.
They begin to dance,
They hop and twirl,
But they are floating in the air,
Gently and gracefully.
But are they real?
They couldn't be.
The old road was closed many years ago.
Maybe they are legends?
I guess we shall never know.
For there is no road through the woods.

Brooke Theis (9)
Halstead Prep School

THE MAGICAL UNICORN

A beautiful waterfall.
The water is gushing.
The horizon is full of pink, yellow and red colours.
Like a pink blossom tree or a red fire flaming in the night.
Then something leapt behind me.
I just took a glimpse of it.
And there in the misty trees, stood a white unicorn gleaming in
the early morning.
She had a white body with pink, rosy cheeks and a tail that sparkled
in the light.
On her delicate head was a horn, like a snowy-white snake,
Sleeping gracefully on her head.
On her feet were golden hooves, flashing like a bolt of lightning.
In the dark, gloomy forest she was eating red wild berries.
After that, she went to the stream for some cold, icy, blue water to
drink.
I looked back at the horizon and saw the bright sun had come out.
When I looked back at the unicorn, she was slowly disappearing
And suddenly I couldn't see her again.

Cassandra Mason (10)
Halstead Prep School

Closed-Down Market

They closed-down the market
Seventy years ago
There used to be people running around in excitement
But now there is nobody
There used to be people selling items
But now there is nobody
There used to be people calling . . .
Running . . .
Shouting . . .
But now there is absolutely nobody
The only noise now is the wind
Blowing around coke cans and crisp packets
I wonder . . .
Was there ever any life there?
I shudder to think
That people would have been calling . . .
Running . . .
Shouting in excitement,
Seventy years ago
Now it is deserted
There used to be happiness
But now only sadness
I hear a creepy echo from somewhere far away
Fruit and vegetables only one pound
I shuddered . . .
It's only a shut-down market from
Seventy years ago.

Becky Lane (9)
Halstead Prep School

If The Sun Were A . . .

If the sun were a flower it would be
A bright, beautiful tulip glistening in the sunlit dew.

If the sun were a fruit it would be
A ripe, round orange hanging patiently
Near to a silently flowing waterfall.

If the sun were a balloon it would float
In the dazzling sky
And drift into a wall of airy cotton wool clouds.

If the sun were a light it would be
A flickering chandelier high up
On a gleaming ceiling.

If the sun were an animal it would be
A roaring, raging lion
Firing heat ferociously.

If the sun was an instrument
It would be a smashing cymbal.

If the sun was a meal it would be
An oozing pancake simmering
In a fabulous, frying pan.

If the sun were a button,
It would be a gold sequinned button
Sewn onto the finest clothes.

If the sun were a person it would be
A happy girl with a marvellous
Magnificent manner in everything she does.

Chloe Birch (10)
Halstead Prep School

READY STEADY - GULP

Butterflies beat tummy
Nails shrink as I bite them
I shiver with fear and cold
Brain is numb
Suddenly
Bang! The gun fires
As I dive gracefully in
I gasp for air as my fingertips touch water
The cheers are muffled
Chlorine fills my nose and ears
Come up to breathe
Hear screams and shouts all around
I look up
The poolside is only inches away
Lungs expand
Hand stretches
Fingers touch
Yes!
Somebody kneels down to pull me out
Gasping for breath
Relief floods my body
I stand up
A medal glistens around my neck
A shiny cup in my hand
A whoop of happiness
Inside me
People whistle, cheer and clap
My photo taken for the sports magazine
Famous
At last!

Elizabeth Kelly (10)
Halstead Prep School

A UNICORN

I saw it.
The sky was blue,
And the clouds were fluffy and white like meringue.
Out of the clouds came a silver unicorn
With a beautiful pinky white horn,
Sparkling in the sunlight.
Its mane was white, flowing in the breeze.
Its wings were pearly as they glinted in the sunlight.
Its eyes were like sky blue pearls.
It glided down towards me
And landed under pink blossom,
And began eating the clean fresh grass.
Its eyes were sparkling in the sunlight.
The blossom fell gracefully to the ground.
Its white tale swishing in the wind.
Slowly it glided up into the sky.
It winked at me
And disappeared forever!

Rosanna Knottenbelt (9)
Halstead Prep School

THE SILKY SUN

If the sun were a flower it would be
A sunflower bobbing in a warm Italian field of corn.

If the sun were a flower it would be
A beach ball bouncing on the golden silky sand.

If the sun were a face it would be
A naughty lion staring at you.

If the sun were a bowl of paint it would be
A yellow egg yoke with a golden shine.

If the sun were a fruit it would be
A round yellow spotty lemon hanging on a tall green tree.

If the sun were a plate it would be
A golden plate on a golden table.

If the sun were a yarn of wool it would be
A lovely silky feel woven into a woolly jumper.

If the sun were a button it would be
A round button on a golden coat.

Amy Lance (10)
Halstead Prep School

A UNICORN POEM

By the waterfall
With luscious green grass
The rocks around the glistening watershine
Like newly polished shoes
The water shines on me
When something caught my eye
In the mist of the waterfall there was a shape
A shape of a unicorn
It was a silvery bodied unicorn
With a sparkly horn
It picked me up on its back
And we were off
Flying over the rainbow
There were purple mountains
Green fields of green grass
And silvery rivers like snakes
We were soon soaring through the sky
Its horn shimmered and shone in the moonlight
Then we flew right down and glided through the water
We went through so fast that I wasn't wet
The unicorn disappeared into the wildness
I was left alone.

Katy Warham (10)
Halstead Prep School

Nocturnophobia

I am scared of the dark.
Like a stamp is fearful of your tongue
Like a plane is cowardly about clouds
Like a cat is cowed by a dog
Like a rose is terrified by a turtle
Like a dark cloud is anxious about the sun
Like a smile is horrified by a frown
Like a wall is frightened by a bulldozer
Like a target is afraid of the arrow
Like an ear is alarmed by a loud sound
Like a piece of meat is shocked by an eagle
Like a chimney is nervous about a chimney sweep
Like a lid is apprehensive about a hand
Like a fork is panicky about a knife
Like a heart has qualms about cancer
Like a glass shivers with fear when she sees a dishwasher
I am scared of the dark.

Kirstin Cooper (10)
Halstead Prep School

A RIVER POEM

This river is my favourite river,
I come to it every afternoon.

At night I hear it splashing and crashing.
Against the drowned wet banks.

I creep out early and stumble down to the river,
The owl hoots above me in the cedar tree.
I put my finger in the still, calm water.

In the afternoon when the bees are buzzing
And the butterflies are dancing.
I go down to my river,
I put my hot face in the water,
And open my eyes wide,
To see all the little fish darting beneath me.

My river will always be in my heart.

Sophie Fowler-Tutt (9)
Halstead Prep School

THE DESERTED BEACH IN WINTER

The beach was closed down
Seventy years ago
Still I hear the odd voice scream
As they run into the sea
I look up at the cliff tops
Which slowly crumble
As the rain falls on the dirty deserted sand
And the waves get bigger as the
Ghostly voices seem to call on the ghostly beach
And howl at me in the wind.

There comes a flash of light in the air
The ghosts slowly creep away and fall into
The sea as it . . .
Shh . . .
Shh . . .
And the pebbles wash away to the dark
Chattering, cold sea . . .
The beach was closed down seventy years ago.

Ellen Elphick (9)
Halstead Prep School

THE DESERTED BEACH IN WINTER

They shut down the beach seventy years ago,
Because of an accident that happened . . .
Seventy years ago.
All that you'll see are seagulls at the ice cream stand,
The big, dangerous rocks,
The little children's fun fair
And the spirit of the boy in the accident . . .
That happened seventy years ago.
All that you'll hear are the screams of the boy,
The squeals of laughter from the children
And squawks of the seagulls . . .
The wind whistles and
The mist swirls around you and
The sand blows in your face and across the ground.
Whatever you do on your visit to the beach,
Enjoy it . . .
But remember what happened . . . seventy years ago.

Elizabeth Gardner (10)
Halstead Prep School

NOCTURNOPHOBIA

I am afraid of the dark
Like a cat is afraid of a dog
Like hay is nervous of a bale
Like the grass is terrified of a lawnmower
Like a stamp is frightened of a letter
Like a mouse is anxious about a rat.

Like wood is fearful of a cutter
Like a pen is cowardly about the paper
Like people are alarmed by bears
Like paper is shaky over glue.

Like Polly the horse is cowardly over growing up.
Like people are allergic to smoke.
Like paper has qualms over scissors.

Like blue is horrified by black
Like books are apprehensive at being read
Like Amy is cowardly over rice pudding
I am afraid of the dark.

Amy Bowerin (9)
Halstead Prep School

THE MOON

The moon is . . .
A pearl strung on a shiny silver string.
A silver bowling ball being pushed into a world of darkness.
A shimmering smile on a bright happy clown.

A grey stone bridge with a midnight black river running through it.
A mime artist's white face wearing starry clothes.
A bauble hanging on a magnificent green tree in a dark room.
A witch's long curved nail stroking a black cat.

A round block of silvery ice sitting in the ebony of night.
A glass plate on a tablecloth of navy blue with jewels sewn on.
A dolphin jumping out of the dark starry water scattering
shining splashes.
A yarn of silver silk in a basket full of glittering crystals and
black wool.

Abigail Binns (9)
Halstead Prep School

The Deserted Beach In Winter

The beach is always deserted
In the cold winter days
The whistling winds
With ghostly sounds . . .
The swish of the water on the shore.
With little lumps of ice,
When you crack it open
You can hear the whale speak,
And the fish gulping water
With a splash of their tails and fins . . .
The crunching on the pebbles
Where people were standing,
In the summer heat.
Children having a swim
And splashing around shrieking excitedly,
Now the beach is always deserted . . .
In the cold winter's night.

Amy Piercy (9)
Halstead Prep School

UNICORN

It started as a dream
I saw it in the clouds
The unicorn with white fur and ebony-black eyes
She swished and swayed
Then came down
I stared in great amazement
I hopped on and round
I saw fields with corn and wheat
We passed some silver flowers
The tree had lots of leaves
So pretty!
The rivers many boats
With fish swimming along and diving
The sea
Was crystal clear with no waves
Still and frozen in the silver night.

Elly Sams (9)
Halstead Prep School

A Deserted Beach In Winter

They closed the beach seventy years ago.
The old cans rattling about,
The edge of the frozen sea.
The spider's web hanging from a rock.
The laughter in the air and broken glass everywhere.
Empty suncream bottles in every place.
The good old times have gone on the beach on a
summer's day.
It's so empty, the pine needles crackle on the beach shore.
The invisible footsteps of a ghost comes nearer.
The gulls fly high, looking for their prey.
The only sound of waves ripple . . .
They closed the beach seventy years ago.

Sarah-Jayne K Stamper (9)
Halstead Prep School

The Lion

This fierce lion with teeth like iron,
Cleverly stalks its prey through the grass,
It spies with eyes like stainless glass.

Then this genius thinks
Now is the time,
And pounces with a roar from behind!

Before he dies,
This prey gawks at this beast with eyes open wide,
And the lion takes this warthog home for a feast.

Sam May (10)
Horsell CE Primary School

LIONS

They stand proudly, big as a bear,
But as sneaky and sly as a fox.
The hunting queen of the forest,
Prowls slowly towards her prey.

The king of the jungle,
The biggest of all,
Cries out to his friends,
With an almighty roar.

He is silky and bright,
With a long shaggy mane.
Golden threads of silk,
Glinting in the African sun.

Back to the queen, the princess, the hunter
Ears pricked, ready to pounce.
On a vulnerable buffalo,
Grazing contentedly away from its herd.

She springs from her pads,
The buffalo spots her,
He tries to run
But she's upon him.

In a flashing of teeth,
And a ripping of claws,
The mighty buffalo
Stands no more.

Jessica Burrowes (11)
Horsell CE Primary School

THE LION

Razor-sharp teeth, as sharp as the rock that could sink a ship
Sly and sleek, stalking his prey.
Cunning and courageous, hunting every day
Sleeping in the golden rays of the sun.
After a diamond day's hard work is done.

The lord of all landscape
Guarding his empire, alert, then he roars.
He stretches his enormously powerful claws.
He is noble to his own but, terrifying to a different kind.
That is why he is the king, to all the beasts of the wild.

Christopher Purvis (10)
Horsell CE Primary School

MY CAT POEM

I have a cat, who travels in a hat.
His name is Pete,
He's rather sweet,
But he's got very stinky feet.

I have a cat, who travels in a hat,
He has a good eye,
Which he uses to spy,
And when he gets tired, he has a nice lie.

I have a cat, who travels in a hat,
He purrs very loud,
It's a humming sound,
But you should hear him when food's around.

I have a cat, who travels in a hat,
But then one day he ran away.

Michele Rice (11)
Horsell CE Primary School

A Wild Cat!

I'd like to be a wild cat,
And treat myself to a mangy rat.
It just occurred to me it was a gerbil.
And then I squeaked and 'puked' a furball.

Now I see a little mouse,
Crawl into the door of a house.
And suddenly I smelt a cat food smell,
And told the mouse to go to Hell.
Now I'm crawling to the bowl of food,
But told myself I'm not in the mood.

I'd like to be a wild cat,
And treat myself to a mangy rat.
Birds flying,
Rats dying,
I love the life of a wild cat.

Curtis Hylton (10)
Horsell CE Primary School

The Night Cat

It is a tiger,
An evil fox-like creature,
Its eyes blaze out like two bright stars,
When it pounces it flies through the air
Like an arrow that never misses,
No one has ever seen it,
It will never be seen,
It is the night cat!

Robert Prince (10)
Horsell CE Primary School

THE KING OF SAFARI

As the King of Safari
Swishes his tail like an angry whip,
He glances slyly around,
With forceful grip.

The striped horses graze slowly on,
Without a care,
In the glowing heat of the sun.
But do they know
What's hidden below,
In the jungle of Africa,
In the undergrowth?

The padded paws
O' the undoubtable king,
Edged with claws,
Under the vulture's wing.

He bends down low,
His shoulderblades high,
His blazing eyes aglow,
Now the vultures fly.

He pounces onto the unsuspecting horse,
And rips it up,
Into a three main course.

He roars out loud with great desire,
As the horses scramble away,
For his head looks like angry red fire.

As he feasts on his prize,
In the distance a hyena lies,
Ready to howl one of his vile cries.

Alice Spencer (11)
Horsell CE Primary School

BLACK CATS

Sneaky black cats,
Wander in the cold like
Snowflakes sprinkling down.

Sneaky black cats,
Pounce like elastic bands
Springing off.

Sneaky black cats,
Has eyes like
Candles glistening
In the dark.

Sneaky black cats,
Have whiskers like
Long dangly hair.

Sneaky black cats,
Sneaky black cats,
Sneaky black cats,
Are very sneaky.

Laura Bradbury (10)
Horsell CE Primary School

THE HUNTER

The cat was born a hunter,
A hunter have I seen?
One little pathetic fur ball,
Grooming with its paws for a little gleam.
Though it climbs the curtains,
Fights like a queen,
The little domestic house cat
A hunter I have seen!

William Sadler (10)
Horsell CE Primary School

Who Is This?

Who is this elusive creature
This fearless hunter, this valiant gymnast?
Who is this sly, sneaking, stalking mouser
This aggressive feline, this swift assassin?

Who is this fluffy fur ball
This warm companion, this couch potato?
Who is this inactive, purring, lazy lounger,
This idle dreamer, this sleepyhead?

It's a cat of course!

Mark Foster (11)
Horsell CE Primary School

The Neglected Cat

Tiddles the helpless cat,
Lying in the garden, resting,
And as the sun shone down in rays,
A poor, helpless cat lies.

Tiddles the helpless little cat,
Got up to go inside,
There was no one there,
'Feed me!' a helpless cat cried.

Some sick people find this funny,
But another case of animal cruelty,
Is something it definitely did not deserve.

Kian Henry (11)
Horsell CE Primary School

Garden Cat

Sleek tiger
Slides through the bushes,
Slinks through the grass,
Stalking his territory,
Stalking the squirrels;
Then streaks of grey and orange on green.
Stealing the birds,
A flutter of feathers left on the grass.
Skylarking with the wind tossed leaves -
A spring, a leap, a stretch into the air.

David Oliver (10)
Horsell CE Primary School

Mr Lion

Mr Lion with big blue eyes,
keeps on eatin' all the pies.
'Naughty lion, naughty lion!' my mother cries.

He tries to tell the truth but he always lies,
because he loves his carrot pies.
Naughty lion, naughty lion, with big blue eyes.

Naughty lion, naughty lion, as fierce as can be,
wolfs down his crumpets,
and sips his tea.

Charis Rokins (11)
Horsell CE Primary School

Cattitude

The murderous mind of a cat
Can take out a bird just like that
The claws as sharp as a blade
For killing birds they made.

Eyes change by day and night
He will be ready for a fight.
Down the back alley it walks.
One day it will be having a fight
And a dog will come along, that serves it right!

Connor Hargreaves (10)
Horsell CE Primary School

Cats

Cats are black,
Cats are white,
Cats like hunting in the night.

Cats are sneaky,
Cats are sleek,
Cats like playing in the heat.

Cats are loyal,
Cats are sweet,
Cats like eating lots of meat.

Cats like hunting for their prey,
Then they sleep throughout the day.

Katy Rhodes (10)
Horsell CE Primary School

CATS

Cats.
What are cats?
Are they fun?
Are they loveable?
Are they annoying?
They are majestic, handsome, wild.
They leap through the air with pride and vanity,
camouflaged with the night sky.

Wait!
A bird!
Cat kneels down waiting for the bird to fly up.
It flies, cat pounces!

The predator catches the prey.
The cat walks through the catflap with a dead robin
in its mouth.
What are cats?
They are themselves.

James Farrier (10)
Horsell CE Primary School

MARMALADE

To see her walking through the evergreen bushes,
It just brings me pure delight,
To feel her silky soft fur running through my fingers,
She purrs like a baby's toy play rattle,
As she sunbathes in the scorching sun,
It seems that her fur is getting softer and softer,
She runs around trying to catch a strand of wool,
Her claws are gleaming like sharp daggers,
Shining eyes darting about like cheetahs,
She pounces grabbing the wool trying to eat it,
She is as determined as a wild cat,
Now she is a plump marmalade fur ball again,
Sleeping so calmly as if she had no animal side,
But come again another day,
She will be a wild cat again!

Anna Westgate (10)
Horsell CE Primary School

The Midnight Cat

Creeping and crawling throughout the moonlit sky,
paws like padded cushions treading
while shadows pass by.
Pouncing from wall to wall,
leaping on telephone wire legs
letting out his screeching call.
Weaving his tail up and around,
making peculiar silhouettes
like a weak snake flat on the ground.
Ears like foxes,
eyes like glowing marbles,
nose like a rose quartz stone,
whiskers like nylon thread,
stomach like a dangling pillow,
claws like little elephant tusks.
What could it be, a cat? . . . the midnight cat.

Gemma Cook (10)
Horsell CE Primary School

Ollie

You can hear the jingle of his bell
The constant miaow of his hunger
Then a sleepy yawn of comfort
He is asleep.

You can hear the purr of his love
Echoing through the darkness
Fluffy tail like a feather duster
Soft, silky fur.

You cannot hear the sound that wakes him
Opening narrow eyes glowing like stars
Moving slyly to catch his prey
Mice, birds beware.

Kimberley Reygadas (11)
Horsell CE Primary School

Garfield The Cat

Some cats are skinny
Some cats are fat
Some cats look like a living room mat.

Some are freaky
Some are sneaky
Cats can be soft and cuddly
But can hiss and spit suddenly.

The cat I like best is my cat in a vest
He keeps me company in the dead of night
When I wake up with a terrible fright.

The cat I admire is Garfield
My orange fluffy friend.

Evan Bowen (10)
Horsell CE Primary School

CATS!

Eyes! Eyes!
Why are cats' eyes like glowing marbles?
Why do they glow?
Don't ask me! I don't know!

Fur! Fur!
Soft, gentle, silky fur,
You could sit there all day just stroking its silky fur.

Paws! Paws!
Why are their paws like cushions walking?
Paws like velvet.

Tails! Tails!
Swinging back and forward.
Tails are like feathery dusters.
Why are their tails like that?
Don't ask me! I don't know!

Ears! Ears!
Pointy ears
Why are their ears like fox's ears?
Hopefully they can hear their fears.

Bodies! Bodies!
Some cats are skinny,
Some cats are fat.
Why are cats fat?
You can ask me! I know!
Why!
Why are cats like that.
I don't know! So don't ask me!
Why are cats like that!
Because that's the way they are!

Emma Rawlings (11)
Horsell CE Primary School

CATS

I wouldn't go down a dark alley at night
A bunch of cats having a fight
Prowling around the street
Treading carefully on soft feet.
Soft, wet, black noses sniffing in bin bags,
They scatter when men come smoking fags.
Waiting for the bird he pounces
Cats run over with little bounces.
They get in a fight over it
Angrily backing away they spit
Hissing pouncing on each other.
The child in the house runs to its mother
Peering out of the window into the night sky.
The cats quickly manoeuvre their bodies into holes to spy
Their eyes glowing in the night.
Their black and white coats glow in the moonlight,
Running back to Furn's flat
Furn rolls over and over on his front door mat
Those teeth have committed murder
But that is the life of a cat.

Scott Maher (10)
Horsell CE Primary School

CATS

Silky, smoothly through the open window,
Leaping across from wall to wall,
Tail waving lazily in the sunshine,
Not a sound to be heard.

Green eyes gleaming in the night-time alleyway,
Black velvet paws never leaving a mark,
Patiently waiting for a mouse to emerge,
Not a sound to be heard.

Razor-sharp claws scratching against the doormat,
Sharp, pointy ears, never missing a pin drop,
Swiftly padding across the hallway,
Not a sound to be heard.

Softly leaping through the doorway,
To its secret hiding place,
Curling up into a ball of warmth,
Not a sound to be heard.

The cat is fast asleep,
Dreaming of the day to come,
Purring loudly to itself,
The silence is broken, a sound is heard!

Louise Sellars (10)
Horsell CE Primary School

CATS

Black cats, white cats,
All very cute.
Ginger cats, golden cats,
All very sweet.

Witches' cats, family cats,
All very furry.
A soft sweeping tail cat,
All very soft.

Nice cats, nasty cats,
All much the same.
Moving with swift elegance,
Soft purring as it sweeps past you.

Soft fluffy, cute, sweet, cuddly,
What's this awful sound?
Cats fighting on the ground.

Maybe, might be, not all very nice,
Always fighting, always glaring.
With coal-black eyes
Fiery evil eyes
Ready to prance!

Matthew Goodey (10)
Horsell CE Primary School

CATS

Cats, eyes like deadly green slits,
Cats, black button nose,
Cats, ears pricked up,
Cats are fascinating, cats are cool,
Cats are cute and cats rule.

Slinking down the alleyway in a royal prance,
Cats, velvet-touch paws,
Cats, fur as soft as satin,
Cats are fascinating, cats are cool,
Cats are cute and cats rule.

Cats, rubbing themselves along your legs,
Cats, lazing on your lap purring softly,
Then turning on you with a screech like car brakes,
Razor-sharp claws come your way.

Cats are fascinating, cats are cruel,
Cats are cute and cats rule.

Shona Probert (11)
Horsell CE Primary School

CATS

They don't care
Creeping, crawling, in the streets at night
Seeing mysterious shadows,
Still no fright,
Sneaking by with those great gloomy eyes,
Like illuminous marbles,
Big furry bodies,
Mostly always getting soggy,
For catching birds, sun or rain,
They don't care.

Nothing to wear, but that big black furry coat,
A rumbling purr,
Always having cat fights, him or her,
They don't care.

When cats run about
With their tail swifting like a snake,
A squeaking miaow, when they are sad,
A happy purr, when they are glad,
Sleeping anywhere,
They don't care.

Jack Coffey (10)
Horsell CE Primary School

Cats

You can hear the desperate cry,
As one of three friends pretend to die,
It's all a game,
But it sounds so real,
It's always for food,
I open the door and shoo them away,
And close the door again.

I go downstairs,
My cat was ice skating,
Across the kitchen floor.
Its hairs up like hedgehog's spikes,
As he gets a fright,
And hits the kitchen door.

My cat's main hobby is digging his claws in
And climbing a tree,
Or ripping the sofa like a child unwrapping a present.

But all cats are different like you and me,
So you don't know what happens next,
Or do you?

Rebecca Challis (10)
Horsell CE Primary School

Security Cats

Some cats are wild,
Some cats are sweet,
Some cats run,
Some cats walk,
Some cats are black,
Some cats attack,
Some cats purr,
Some cats have fur,
Some cats patrol the streets,
Tiptoeing on padded feet.

Sam Smith (10)
Horsell CE Primary School

Cats!

Cats are so cute,
Cats can be mean,
Make sure that he doesn't get seen,
Pouncing around trying to find food,
Oh no, he's caught another bird.

Whipping tail like a lace of leather,
Lots of soft fur like a ton of feathers,
Whiskers like toothpicks, grass or sticks,
Paws like such little pillows.

Ears like a fox,
He purrs like a man snoring,
Cries like a wild bear that keeps on roaring.

Alice Cross (10)
Horsell CE Primary School

My Cat's Flowers

My cat is really fat,
Her eyes are like green gems,
But when she's outside,
Where are the flowers' stems?

My cat you see,
Hates music in any key,
But in her mind,
The flowers have powers,
So she has to kill all of mine.

One sunny day,
There were no flowers left,
So brought our cat a bit of a zest.

My cat's flowers are now really ours,
And now all she does is purr,
We think?

But now we know,
She's grown out of that phase,
And she's lost all her fat,
But now she's after my pet rat.

Jamie Squelch (10)
Horsell CE Primary School

A Cat's Day Out

The sleek movement of a cat
Shocks me in a way
Where it moves with its paws
And it grabs with its sharp claws.

The sleek movement of a cat
Shocks me in a way
Being chased by a dog
And climbing up the tree's log.

The sleek movement of a cat
Shocks me in a way
Climbing across the wall
Jumping from garden to garden evermore.

Richard Hylton (10)
Horsell CE Primary School

Katz

The piercing eye of an unaware victim,
The slow meander of the cat,
The mouse lies down, this it will regret,
The cat leaves it dead by the mat.

The slick silky sleek of the raptor,
Like a snake slithering to lunch,
As she followed the mouse she intended to catch,
Abbey caught the mouse, that's my hunch.

The long curling roller coaster of a tail,
The beautiful button black nose I spy,
As the cats bounce happily,
They look like they were bound to fly.

Chris Wallis (11)
Horsell CE Primary School

Cats

Their wide eyes like two blazing fires,
These cats everyone admires.

Soft fluffy coats like sheep's fur,
All day long they purr and purr.

Most of the time they sleep,
Except for night when they creep.

They go out on the street,
Walking along on their velvety feet.

Climbing up trees jumping on walls,
Balance is vital in case it falls.

My cat chases lots of mice,
He thinks the taste is very nice.

Morgan Rimay-Muranyi (10)
Horsell CE Primary School

MOLLY

Round soft paws swiftly moving,
Like soft blue velvet shoes.
Walking around with her silky soft fur,
Like a new blue satin dress.
With her strong sharp claws she struts about,
Like long, thin fingernails but on the ground.
The flickering light in her vicious eyes.
Like sparks about to start a fire.
Her ears twitch when she hears the faintest sound
Like a woman being followed in the night.
She screeches when she is in danger
Like a person just been caught with a fright.
But the one thing that makes her happy,
Is when you stroke her and she purrs all night.

Henna Ahmed (11)
Horsell CE Primary School

THAT OLD TABBY CAT

That old tabby cat doesn't do much,
With mittened paws and an autumn coat,
Her name's Tammy that beautiful cat,
Sitting on a rough doormat.

But what does she do at night?

Leaps across the moon from house to house,
Like an elegant model,
Quickly pouncing on her good friend Chess,
Saying, 'The sun is rising, let's go home,
Until they all get up.'

Tammy howls like a pack of wolves
Wanting her to come,
We do not know who she is,
But we know she's a good friend of Tammy and Chess.

That cool tabby cat does do much,
With a silky tail swaying to the beat,
Her name's Tammy that elegant cat,
Sitting on a roof in the moonlight.

When she fights she's a real boxer,
With a whip and a scratch from her rusty claws,
A high-pitched screech like a car's handbrake,
Tammy's a boxer; she gets up to things at night,
We love her so; her fur's like velvet and she's lovely to squeeze.

Susannah Schrock (10)
Horsell CE Primary School

TWO FACED

My cat at home is soft and silky,
as careful and delicate as can be,
padding around inquisitively,
searching out everywhere,
then playing with me.

But when I leave, it slinks out,
to carry on a second life,
on the street a killer lurks,
uncovering sabre from the velvet pads,
menacing eyes a demon unleashed.

Ready to kill in an instant,
prepared to do anything to survive,
a bird, a mouse, anything will do,
trained to kill straight away,
why my cat so kind and gentle.

Lawrence Barrott (11)
Horsell CE Primary School

WINTER'S WHITE

White, white, it's winter's special word.
White snow twinkling from the air.
Trees are bare, leaves have fallen,
White icicles hang from rooftops like spear heads.
Pale winter sun makes them gleam like diamonds.
Jack Frost has turned paths into white sparkling skating rinks.
Children are throwing snowballs having a great time,
While the snow is here.
Snowmen stand watching them.
Winter's white, winter's white.

Aaron McDonald (9)
Mytchett Primary School

REVENGE

First Witch
Cackling around cauldron chuck in . . .
Bat's wing,
Lung of dog,
Wart's skin,
Polluted water from a bog,
Make this potion what it's worth,
Throw in a fungi log,
Make Spike have a new birth!

All
Revenge is sweet, good is sour,
This potion cast within the hour.
Let no happiness be upon, be upon the lives
Of people who in happiness thrive.

Second Witch
Now it is the main course
Ingredients of utter remorse
Claw of cat
Nightmares of the night
Disease of rat
Soldiers violent fight
Claw of crab
Sharks fin
Blood from a stab
The truth we'll spin.

Chorus.

Charlotte Crabb (11)
Mytchett Primary School

Witches' Spell

Hop, skip, turn around
Watch out or you'll be a hound

Jam from your toes,
Bogies from your nose
Toad so green
And a gory spleen.
Sand from a baby's nappy
A laugh so happy.

Hop, skip, turn around,
Watch out or you'll be a hound.

Fat maggots crawling,
A baby is bawling
An eagle's wing
And a bumblebee's sting
A scale from a fish,
And mould from a dish,
A button from a coat,
Sail from a boat.

Harriet Cooper (10)
Mytchett Primary School

Wicked Witches

First Witch
In thy house, around cauldron go,
Pass it, shake it, drop and throw.
Poison ivy, thee must die,
Ha, we three witches must lie.
Burn it, steam it, make it hot,
Macbeth must drink the lot!

Double, double, toil and trouble,
Fire burn, and cauldron bubble.

Second Witch
Stem of plant and weed of grass,
Mix it in to make it class.
Cobra's breath and a rat's bite,
An owl's sharp watch, in the night.
A spider's eye and frogs' leg
Mixed together in a keg.

Double, double, boil and trouble.
Fire burn and cauldron bubble.

Lindsey Parker (10)
Mytchett Primary School

Night

In the silence of night
There is nothing but darkness surrounding
Imagining thoughts of what's 'not there
Sends chills down your spine,
Thumps, bangs, chills around,
Senses light being driven away.
The reaper of night comes to haunt,
Nothing your mind can do but surrender.
The dawn comes the next day, ready to rule once again.

Sofie Kent (10)
Mytchett Primary School

Unleashed Spirits Rise

First Witch
Lonely spirits of the night,
Jealousy, anger, fear and spite
Nightmares dark and very mean,
Twisted souls put in a bean
Smelly socks and scaly skin,
In the cauldron it goes in.

All
Double, double, toil and trouble,
Fire burn, and cauldron bubble.

Second Witch
Spot of cheetah, beak of bird,
Something that cannot be heard
Shell of tortoise, howl of dog,
Cold shiver of winter's fog
Silent scream of a schoolgirl,
When the teacher's eyes start to swirl.

Bobbie Owen (11)
Mytchett Primary School

THIRD VERSE

Bat's fang teeth,
A dead man's wreath.
In the pot we all throw,
Puppy tails, toads' tongues,
And entrails go.
Throw them all into the pot,
Stir them round and make them hot.
Under moon that shines so bright
Mid the darkness of the night.
Wizard's wart and dragon's breath,
Will lead the king unto his death.

Sarah Byrnes (11)
Mytchett Primary School

BLACK HOLE

In the void of space,
Light has an enemy.
Its belly endless,
And hunger never-ending.

The revolving trap,
Of evil black darkness.
Whirls threads of deceit,
On its helpless victims.

The mount of gravity,
Barely in our dimension.
On the event horizon,
A gravity well.

A black hole!

Daniel Balmbra (10)
Mytchett Primary School

AUTUMN

I wake up in the morning and look out of my window.
I see mist in the distance and the dew on the grass down below.
The leaves are falling to the ground like a small gentle tornado
Whizzing round and round.

Squirrels scurry through the trees
Looking for nuts beneath the leaves.
Birds migrating, animals hibernating,
While the wind is howling on a cold, frosty night.

Autumn brings the cold, windy and frosty mornings,
The crispy leaves and the bare, barky trees.
I smell a lovely smell; and rush outside.
There in front of me is a homemade loaf of bread.
So I get ready for a warm supper.

Kathryn Roke (9)
Mytchett Primary School

TORTOISE

Slow movers,
Veggie hoover.

Silent creature,
Pretty feature.

Hard shell,
No smell.

Lives years,
No fears.

Unusual pet,
Nice to get!

Michael Newland (11)
Mytchett Primary School

Four Seasons

S pring weather appears now,
P ussy cats call out miaow.
R ainbows in the blue sky,
I n morning birds sing and fly.
N uts from squirrels all around,
G roaning and moaning animals around.

S ummer weather appears now,
U nderneath the rainbows people say, 'Wow!'
M ornings come very bright,
M oving animals on a dark night.
E venings come and it's very light,
R ainbows are a beautiful sight.

A utumn weather appears now,
U nderneath the grass are creatures, wow.
T rees end up with no leaves,
U nderneath the grounds are buried leaves.
M uddy puddles along the road,
N aughty animals hide like a toad.

W inter weather appears now,
I really don't know how.
N ight-time very comes soon,
T ill then we have the moon.
E ntering snow falls down from the sky.
R ain in the clouds is up so high.

Melissa Plom (10)
Mytchett Primary School

SPELL

Third Witch
Eye calls ''tis time 'tis time.'

First Witch
Round and round we run and run
Fulfilling our dreams and having fun.
Mixing bits of a child's toe
With eyes and ears of frogs and newts
Put in a cauldron and boil like soup.

All
Winter swirl, water bubble
Make this spell start all the trouble.

Second Witch
Add three people to reveal the spell
Add the contents of a bell
Add a zombie's fingernail
With a little puppy tail.
Death departs, the spell is done
Death to children is going to be fun.

All
Water swirl, water bubble,
Make this spell start all the trouble.

Jake White (11)
Mytchett Primary School

What If . . .

What if . . .
Children could drive cars
Anywhere they like, at any speed they like
But that will never happen.

What if . . .
Money grew on trees
Everyone will be happy and rich
But that will never happen.

What if . . .
Sweets and chocolates were free
All the children will enjoy it until their teeth fall out
But that will never happen.

What if . . .
You only have to go to school for three days
Children will learn what they need to know
That could happen!

Ryan Howson (9)
Mytchett Primary School

We Wash In The Sewer

We wash in the sewer
With bits of dirt and anything we can spot.

For it suits everyone and we find it fun
When the water is greasy and hot.

It's a funny idea, not to use water that is clear,
It's really strange we know.

But you can't beat the treat of washing your feet
In someone's overflow.

Ryan Wells (10)
Mytchett Primary School

Wind

Wind is like the Earth's guardian
It can go anywhere it likes
It blows through hair and leaves freely
It sets the speed of sound.

In spring it rushes past leaf buds,
And blows through all the grass,
But turns into a mere breeze
To play with tiny lambs.

In summer it can only slow,
For fear of running out
Of power needed in three months time
For autumn time draws near.

In autumn the leaves are grateful
For the helping hand
The wind is always ready to give
Leaves willing to get to the ground.

In winter the wind is like a different thing,
Tearing and rushing around
Kicking up small splashes of snow,
Uncovering the icy ground.

Laura Hylands (9)
Mytchett Primary School

Snow

Snow, snow, snow, snow
Makes the children's faces glow.
Throwing snowballs at each other
Oops, one just hit my mother.

Chorus
Snow, snow, snow, snow,
Snow, snow, snow, snow.

Snow, snow, snow, snow
When the wind goes blow, blow.
Building snowmen one by one
Having lots and lots of fun.

Chorus

Snow, snow, snow, snow,
Tingly fingers, tingly toes.
What will happen next
In the snow?

Chorus.

Abbi Field (9)
Mytchett Primary School

The Countryside

T he tractor roars as it harvests wheat.
H orses gallop through the wind.
E verywhere is quiet.

C ars don't normally come here.
O n the hill stands a tree rustling.
U nderground worms wriggle.
N obody is seen for ages except the farmer.
T rees hide a magical world.
R oses overflow with colour.
Y ou can see the fabulous things.
S ome people visit the village.
I n the grass animals scatter.
D on't destroy this place with litter.
E at the fresh vegetables from the ground.

Away from crowds, away from cars
Peace and quiet, at last.

Daniel Hardman (10)
Mytchett Primary School

MY MAGIC BOX

(Based on 'Magic Box' by Kit Wright)

I will put in my box . . .
My last memory of Legoland
All the tasty sweets you could get
A sparkly silvery seal that is hurt.

I will put in my box . . .
The heart of my special mum and dad
The kindness out of my sister
All the money I get for my birthday.

My box is made . . .
Of chocolate and golden leaves
One side is for money
One side is for a family tree
One side is for friends
And the other is for something special.

Natasha Ward (10)
Mytchett Primary School

WEATHER

R ain comes down in buckets
A nimals run for cover
I nsects hide in holes
N oise raindrops fall.

S unny sun shines bright
U mbrellas not needed
N ice glittering hot sun shines.

S now is falling on the ground
N ice and soft as can be
O h! it is wonderful
W hite snowdrops slowly fall.

W ild wind blows
I n the falling leaves
N ow the trees are bare
D o you like the wild wind.

Zoë Filshie (9)
Mytchett Primary School

AUTUMN MORNING

Autumn, autumn, it is coming
As the leaves hurtle to the ground.
When the squirrels scurry through the grass,
Searching for food before they hibernate.

A windy day as the squirrels scurry
As they run very fast in a hurry.
They find some nuts and take them back to their tree,
They find warmth and stay there for night.

Autumn, autumn, it is coming
As the leaves hurtle to the ground.
When the squirrels scurry through the grass,
Searching for food before they hibernate.

James Hagan (9)
Mytchett Primary School

MAGIC BOX

(Based on 'My Box' by Kit Wright)

I will put in the box . . .
A gold bar the size of a building
A ruby-red car with five engines and gold exhaust pipes.
A silver robot that sparkles in the sun and collects my meals
for me every day.

I will put in the box . . .
Some juicy fruit that tastes like the sweetness from Heaven
A pad with pages of gold
A drink of hot chocolate with silky bubbles overflowing the top
A box of lovely milk chocolate biscuits that never ends.

My box is made of diamond with a little golden castle on the top.
It has ruby hinges with blue spikes on each side.

Alexander Barlow (10)
Mytchett Primary School

LEAVES

Autumn has come again
The leaves turn from green to red, amber, gold and brown.
When the wind blows the leaves,
Leaves scatter all over the place swishing and swirling,
Twisting and turning.
Then falling gently to the ground.

Children come to play gathering the leaves,
They jump and run through them, listening to the autumn sounds.
As they *crunch, crackle* and squash underfoot
Children try to catch the falling leaves, so they can make a wish.
What do you wish for?

The sun shines through the trees making the leaves shine like jewels.
Making the parks look like a magical dream of our own.
Dogs search and scatter the leaves to find the sticks and balls
That their owners have thrown
I love the autumn do you?

We search for chestnuts in the leaves
But find hedgehogs curled up snug and warm ready for the long winter.
I love the autumn because of all the falling coloured leaves,
And the beautiful breeze rustling through my hair, don't you?

Bromwyn Brett (9)
Mytchett Primary School

MAGIC BOX

(Based on 'Magic Box' by Kit Wright)

I will put in my box . . .
A sparkling camera that lights up the world.
A flash of the golden star making a wish.
A glimpse of the eclipse.

I will put in my box . . .
The shiny shark that lights up the sea.
The sparkling sun glitters in the sky.
The skin of a slithering snake.

I will put in my box . . .
The silver dolphin jumping in the Arctic ocean.
The snowman slowly evaporating in my garden.
The fur of a white polar bear exploring the Arctic.

My box is fashioned with beaming red and blue rubies
With a golden background and silver hinges like sharks' teeth.

Marc Simmonds (9)
Mytchett Primary School

IN MY BOX

(Based on 'Magic Box' by Kit Wright)

I will put in my box . . .
A glittering bright star from up in the dark night sky,
And a secret that will never be told (*sshhh*).

I will put in my box . . .
A magical land from far, far away,
And a beautiful gold diamond ring.

I will put in my box . . .
A wizard that can tell the future,
And a swarm of buzzing bees.

I will put in my box . . .
The ticking of a clock
And a *bang!* of a firework.

I will hide in my box . . .
For ever and ever,
And nobody will find me.

Katie Patterson (9)
Mytchett Primary School

My Magic Box

I will put in the box . . .
A sparkling unicorn with glittering horns
A giant chocolate bar with cream in it
A sports car that roars like a tiger.

I will put in my box . . .
A hundred pound T-shirt with sparkles on it
A dress with real gold around it
A little hamster with plaits on it.

My box is . . .
Gold with sequins on it
Moons and stars at the bottom
Unicorns for the stands.

Nicola Gallop (10)
Mytchett Primary School

Ice Cream

I like ice cream, oh such a lot
It is good when days are hot.

Vanilla, chocolate, strawberry flavour
It will boost your happy behaviour.

It makes me cold,
But hopefully they won't all be sold.

Ice cream, ice cream makes me happy
And doesn't make me very snappy.

It is fun to eat
It will give you a real good treat!

Charlotte Lindley (10)
Mytchett Primary School

FOOTBALL

It's early morning,
Mum calls my name as I stir,
I think of my game.
The sun is out, the day is bright, I hope today I get it right.
I'm very slight and not very tall,
But I think I know I can run with the ball.
I go to school dreaming of scoring the winner,
The bell rings out, it's time for dinner.
The teams are picked, we're ready to start,
I hear the pounding of my beating heart.
The game is tight, I need to run,
But by the end I've scored and won.
The other team is down, and beat,
Now it's time to rest my feet.
My kit is muddy and very dirty,
Mum will collect me at three-thirty.
I sit at home thinking of the day I've had,
All I know is I'm better than
Dad!

Josh Kipping (10)
Mytchett Primary School

Snow!

White, soft crunchy sound
It falls light onto the ground.

Chorus
Snow is falling down and down
And melting as it touches the ground.

Snow reminds me of Christmas Day
In the snow the children play.

Chorus

Black eyes and carrot nose
A big smile when it snows.
I build my snowman small or tall
And roll the body and head into a ball.

Chorus

Dominique Quinlan (9)
Mytchett Primary School

THE VIEW FROM OUTSIDE

I can hear . . .
The flying wind,
The singing birds,
And the chattering children.

I can feel . . .
The whistling wind blowing through my soft hair,
The cold breeze on my face,
The aeroplane going through the white fluffy clouds,
And the birds going past my head.

I can see . . .
The beautiful flowers in the blowing breeze,
The green grass on the ground
And the houses in the far distance.

I can smell . . .
The calm and beautiful spring
The scent of daffodils and tulips as they start to grow.

Rebecca Holford (10)
Mytchett Primary School

AUTUMN DAYS

As I snuggle to get out of my bed I am hypnotised by the marvellous smell of freshly baked bread.
I run downstairs as fast as a leopard pursuing its swift prey.
I devour my freshly baked bread and it makes me feel energised for the long autumn day ahead.

I look at my burning fire, I can see sparks sprinkling out.
As the leaves sway in the Arctic gale they shoot to the high sky.
The leaves get darker and darker.
From green they turn to golden-brown.
As the squirrels scurry on the sticky floor,
Their tails get bushier by the second.

Autumn is here, autumn is here once again
No more playing in the park, no more sunshine in the sky.
But most of all no more coloured soft flowers.

Srijit Venkat (10)
Mytchett Primary School

WATERFALL

W is for water *w*eeping
A is for *a*pplauding
T is for water *t*umbling
E is for water *e*rupting
R is for water *r*umbling
F is for water *f*alling
A is for water *a*valanching
L is for water *l*eaping
L is for water *l*ooping.

Jacque Bayliss (8)
New Monument Primary School

AIRPORT

Aeroplanes flying, flight lights
Flashing, passengers dashing,
Doors swinging, shoes stamping,
It's Christmas Eve but not silent night.
Babies crying, guards sleeping,
Floors shining, lights flashing,
Hippies dancing.
It's goodbye but not goodnight.
Children shouting, people chatting,
Toilets flushing, water running.
Windows slamming.
Windows are slamming but
The lightning's striking
It's alright because we're flying tonight.

Shamile Chaudhry (11)
New Monument Primary School

The Noisy Jungle

I was running in the jungle,
When I heard a thundering and smashing
And cracking and clashing noise.
I could hear animals in the jungle roaring
And shouting and screaming.
It was cold in the jungle.
The trees were twirling and twisting and rattling,
As if they were going to break.
I was shivering and shouting and twisting and turning.
The monkeys were jumping tree to tree
Their legs were swinging and turning and twisting.
Their bodies were choking and sizzling.
The tigers roaring and spitting,
And smashing and slapping.

Sara Munir (11)
New Monument Primary School

HULLABALOO

What can we do?
Wolves are howling, growling, roaring,
As rain is splashing, dashing,
Trees swaying, crashing,
Dancing to the whistling wind.

Hullabaloo
Children too are playing
Shouting and running
The chatting from the teacher
And the working.

Hullabaloo

Panting and barking are the dogs
In the dark
The mice running and squeaking
In the rain.

Hullabaloo.

Mohammed Ali (11)
New Monument Primary School

WAR

Making enemies is the worst thing
Like casting a spell like a witch.
There is crying
And too many wanderings.

People are crying and comforting
Cave hiding
Soldiers are celebrating
Also shooting.

People are co-operating
To make future planning
People are escaping
And also running and crawling.

In the end people are hugging
Horrible, terrible war and fighting.

Tapiwa Moyo (11)
New Monument Primary School

River

Splashing and dashing,
Rushing and gushing,
Scattering and pattering,
Tipping and dipping.

There goes the thundering river -
So violently and silver.

There's twisting and twirling,
So quivering and a touch of shivering.

It's clashing like mad,
And slapping so bad.

It's shouting with roar,
As if he won a war.

So suddenly, so silent,
No madness and no violence.

No splashing like a boulder dashing,
No rushing like water gushing.

No scattering like raindrops pattering.
No tipping like a spilt dipping.

No rattling or roaring,
Just nice and smooth and
A bit too boring.

Rubina Miah (11)
New Monument Primary School

Kitchen

There was an old kitchen
with a big fat old lady.
There was . . .
bashing and crashing and moaning
and groaning and lying and crying
and boiling and spoiling
and hissing and spitting
and frying and spying
and steaming and beaming.

Then there was an old kitchen
with a big fat old lady and a skinny
little man and there was . . .
crashing and bashing
and shouting and clouting
and frizzling and sizzling
and banging and slamming
and running and jumping and then . . .
Bang!

Paul Nadeem (10)
New Monument Primary School

Happiness

Happiness is holidays sunny and warm.
Happiness is the smell of soft sweetcorn.
Happiness is me as sweet as can be.
Happiness is the smell of hot warm tea.
Happiness is coconuts from a coconut tree.
Happiness is the buzzing of a bumblebee.

Holly Clarke (9)
Purley Oaks Primary School

TALL TALES

I saw a pirate ship
Sailing through the sea
I saw some ugly pirates
As stupid as can be.

No you never, you never
I did.

I saw a boring rainbow
Its colours, black and white,
It only got its colours back
In the sleepy dead of night.

No you never, you never
I did.

I saw a living dinosaur
Its teeth were big and white.
His green and scaly skin you see
Gave him a licence to fright.

No you never, you never
I did.

I saw your mother
Cleaning your room,
Calling you in
Holding a mop and a broom.

No you never, you never
You did!

Harriet Fiddimore (8)
Purley Oaks Primary School

I Saw

I saw Harry Potter shake hands with Malfoy,
I saw Hermione turn into a witch,
I saw Ron fight with his brother,
I saw Neville fly in the sky,
I saw Dumbledore go in the girls' bathroom,
I saw Wood be captain for ages,
I saw Hogwarts from high above,
I saw Gryffindor win the House Cup.

Krassi Petrova (9)
Purley Oaks Primary School

I've Never Heard The Queen Say 'Thanks'

I've never heard the Queen say 'thanks'
Or hear her sing in rhyme.
I've never 'eard the Queen speak slang,
But I'll watch her next time.
I've never heard the Queen belch,
Or fart in the middle of town.
I've never seen the Queen be sick,
In her dressing gown.
You may not have seen these,
But if you ask the King,
I'm sure he will tell you,
He's seen all these things.

Ben Elliott (8)
Purley Oaks Primary School

THE KING

I've never seen the King laugh
Or chuckle in his chair,
I've never seen him in Tesco's
Buying shampoo for his hair.
I've never seen him on the beach
Laughing without a care
Sitting on a jellyfish eating a pear.
Now I know this sounds quite weird
But if you ask the Queen,
She would probably say that
She has seen:
The King laugh and chuckle in his chair,
She has seen him in Tesco's buying shampoo for his hair.
'I have seen him on the beach
Laughing without a care
He always sits on jellyfish eating a pear.'
And then she added at the end,
'He wriggles in his bed.
So now you have the chance, my love
To be the Queen instead.'

Nathan Shaw (9)
Purley Oaks Primary School

Nonsense Poem

At Christmas in July
Animals live in houses
Animals can speak
Pigs fly
Animals hunt humans.

At Christmas in July
When lights go green cars stop
Babies go to casinos
Tony Blair is in nursery
The Queen is in playschool.

At Christmas in July
Aliens live on Earth
Aliens speak English
Aliens eat the floor
Aliens have cats and dogs.

At Christmas in July
Animals play Monopoly
Time goes backwards
Books read to children
The alphabet goes backwards.

Jordan Giddings (9)
Purley Oaks Primary School

The Big Band

In the big band
The big base drum roars
The tambourine sang a tune
And the noise filled the block.

Music, music all day long.

In the big band
They play the triangle
And play all day
Until the day dies.

Music, music all day long.

In the big band
They march along
Stamp, stamp, stamp,
All day long.

Music, music all day long.

Kiri Moon (8)
Purley Oaks Primary School

I Saw

I saw Nicola pick her toes
I saw a panda picking its nose
I saw it raining cats and dogs
I saw it raining lizards and frogs
I saw flying pigs
I saw them with their wigs
I saw someone shout
I saw them pick their snout.

Rebecca Harvey (9)
Purley Oaks Primary School

I'VE NEVER HEARD THE QUEEN SHOUT

I've never heard the Queen shout
Or seen her trip over her dress.
Or even seen her do her hair
Or seen her make a mess.
I've never seen her close the curtains
If it is sunny.
I've never seen her pick her nose
Or even spend her money.
I've never seen her eyes water
When she eats spice.
I haven't even seen her scream
When she sees some mice
But I bet if I ask the King
He would have seen the Queen
Shout or seen her trip over her dress
Or seen her do her hair.
And he has seen her make a mess,
And he has probably seen her close her curtains
When it is sunny.
And has seen her pick her nose
And he has seen her spend all her money
And he has probably seen her eyes water
When she eats spice.
I bet he has seen her scream when
She sees some mice.
But I haven't
Have you?

Jessica Elsey (9)
Purley Oaks Primary School

Seasons

Here comes winter
Snow falling to the ground
It starts raining, get inside, bye-bye winter!
Here comes spring.
Flowers are blooming, here comes the sun
Here comes the rain, together they will make a rainbow.
Bye-bye spring!
Here comes summer
Time for swimming, no rain this season.
Bye-bye summer!
Last of all, autumn
Leaves are falling again,
Bye-bye autumn!
Back to winter,
It's now the New Year!

Kaitlyn Sheeran (8)
Purley Oaks Primary School

Food, Food

Ross likes eating candyfloss,
Betty likes eating spaghetti,
Ellie likes eating strawberry jelly,
Murray likes eating curry,
Lisa likes eating pizza,
Lee likes eating peas,
Sam likes eating jam,
That man likes eating spam!

Rebecca David (10)
Purley Oaks Primary School

A WEATHER POEM

The rain comes out,
The rain comes out,
I don't want the rain to come out.
The snow comes out,
The snow comes out,
I do not want the snow to come out.
The wind comes out,
The wind comes out,
I do not want the wind to come out.
The moon comes out,
The moon comes out,
I do not want the moon to come out.
The stars come out,
The stars come out,
I do not want the stars to come out.
I want the sun!
I want the sun to come out.

Tahnée Seagrave (7)
Purley Oaks Primary School

CHRISTMAS TIME

Soft snow, hard snow, beautiful snow,
Crispy snow with baby robins jumping about
Robins hop onto Santa's sleigh
He always says: 'Hop, hop, go away.'
The robins sing, 'Jingle Bells,
Jingle all the way.'
Down into the soft snow, ho, ho, ho!

Darcie Kelly (8)
Purley Oaks Primary School

I Want To Make A Sandwich

A nice juicy sandwich
With chocolate bananas,
Carrots, chicken, corn,
Lettuce, radish, potato,
Blackberries, strawberries, pears,
Cherries, grapes, peaches, oranges, too.
Crisps, apricots, plums!
Now that's what I call a
Gorgeous sandwich.

Joanne Matheson (8)
Purley Oaks Primary School

The Romans

The soldiers fight, fight, fight.
They live in forts, where they sleep at night.
And in the day the children play
While adults work not far away.
If you're a slave there's lots to do
Cook, tidy and clean.
If you're rich or an emperor, that's fine,
Sit, relax and drink your wine.
Times are different now,
For us at school or home,
But think what it was like,
Back then in ancient Rome.

Lola Meredith (8)
Purley Oaks Primary School

BEWARE OF THE MAD-BLOODED SHARK!

Deep in the water there is a horrid-blooded shark
It's big, it's vicious, it will tear you up
Into pieces and move from place to place.
His teeth are sharp as a knife
His eyes are round as a circle
He will see you, he will watch you
His mouth will water angrily
You can't see him but he can see you
He will never stop and he will never sleep
All he wants is a nice fresh meat
Bam!
It grabs you
So beware, beware, of the mad-blooded shark.

Marsha Egwea (11)
Purley Oaks Primary School

HAPPY

Happy is a brilliant feeling.
It is like seeing dolphins jumping out of the water.
It is shades of blue, peach and yellow.
It is the sun rising in the sky.
It tastes of chocolate melting in your mouth.
It smells like the scent of flowers in people's gardens.
It feels as if there is sand between your toes.
I like being happy!

Happy!

Natasha McInerney (11)
Purley Oaks Primary School

SMASHING DASHING SKATES

I swing as I sway,
In my smashing
Dashing skates.

Take the candy sprays
They're yummy every day
It's easy peasy
Lemon squeasy to
Rock all night and day.

I zoom down streets
Say hello to
People I meet.

I'm the one
That glides
In my 2-wheel drive
I'm the fastest rider
You'll ever see.

I love the screeching
Under my wheels
But I hate the
Squeaky squeals
'Get out of the way!
Can't you watch
Where you're going?'

I know that they like the show
They just don't like showing it though.

Fiona Dougan (11)
Purley Oaks Primary School

THE CREATURE UNDER MY BED

Green skin
Black hair
Warty body
This is the creature under my bed.

Crooked face
Long thin legs
Bent claws
This is the creature under my bed.

When it is bedtime it reaches out its claw.
I leap into bed, phew it didn't get me.
But it waits till next time.

Holly Burraway Andrews (11)
Purley Oaks Primary School

VAMPIRE HOUSE

A vampire house
It is coated in evil,
The full moon is here.

The evil awakes,
It sends shivers down your spine,
But I see blood trails.

I hear ghostly laughs
I'm scared, the moon is now dark
The evil is here.

Sharn Brown (10)
Purley Oaks Primary School

Horror Haikus

The deserted house
With creepy soft spiderwebs,
This makes you shiver.

A creepy vampire
Awakes into the full moon
Sucking people's blood.

The screaming towers,
Shriek and shout all through the night.
The danger awakes.

The bad school opens
Into the night with bad ghosts,
The bloodsucking starts.

Olivia Procter (11)
Purley Oaks Primary School

The Midnight Race

Curtains pulled back
Car doors opening
To welcome passengers with open arms.
Walking feet starting
To their cars at night
Bright eyes shining
The race begins
Brum, brum
Cars speeding
At the midnight race.

Dyane Baden-Moore (11)
Purley Oaks Primary School

VAMPIRE HAIKUS

Broken cracked windows
Nothing is ever clear now
No one can see in.

I am in trouble
The sound of my pain echoes
I struggle with it.

It tries to bite me
So I will be a vampire
But the light comes up.

Back home, run away
He climbs inside his coffin
For hundreds of years!

Danielle Sheeran (10)
Purley Oaks Primary School

ANGER

Anger is an unpleasant feeling
Like spiders spinning a web,
Like falling into a gruesome swamp.
Anger, let's break it together you and me.
Anger is stopping us in our tracks,
Anger is a disgusting feeling,
Like jumping off a diving board.
Anger gives me restless nights,
Everything seems black and white.
Anger.

Luis Shove (10)
Purley Oaks Primary School

BUT I HAVE TO GO TO THE LOO

Miss Dye won't let me go to the loo
I think I'm seeing things
I don't know what to do
'I really need to go Miss
Believe me I do!'

'Please Miss Dye I've got to go
I really need to go.' Opsy too late
Err! Yuck!
'Sorry.'
'Right now Missy, go get Miss Morry
And start mopping up!'

Hannah Clarke (10)
Purley Oaks Primary School

HAPPINESS

It's a magnificent feeling . . .

Like the sun is above your head
It's the colour orange because orange makes me happy
It's a waterfall on a sunny day
It tastes like a packet of salt and vinegar crisps
It smells like the scent of flowers everywhere
It feels as if you're floating on a lilo in the sea
It's the best feeling you could ever have
And when you do have this feeling take advantage of it.
    Happiness.

Emily Brown (11)
Purley Oaks Primary School

Excitement

Is a great, amazing feeling,
Like you're a balloon that just wants to burst,
It's a bright orange colour.
It is a waterfall you want to jump into.
It tastes like candyfloss you just can't get enough of.
It feels as if you're a volcano just about to erupt.
It's like the sun out at night.
Excitement!

Philippa Mensah (10)
Purley Oaks Primary School

The Midnight Howl Haiku

The full moon is white
And the man has changed again
His fangs drip with blood.

Scott Friel (11)
Purley Oaks Primary School

The House Awakes

The windows open their eyes
The duvet fidgets restlessly
The alarm clock screams
The lights jump on
Water spits out the tap
The kettle blinks
The doorbell sneezes
The regiment of milkbottles stand to attention.

Daisy Milward (10)
Purley Oaks Primary School

THE GRUESOME NIGHT

The phantom's alive
It walked down the creepy hall
It tapped on my door.

The ghost goes past me
It hides in my room somewhere
I spotted the ghost.

The skull is yellow
It stood there on the cupboard
Its spooky eyes glow.

The skeleton danced
It came out of the graveyard
It started to limp.

The alien glides,
It crept, it jerked, it slithered by
It's an alien.

The zombie walked stiff
And creeping alone it limps
Zombie stopped walking.

Aisha Haughton (10)
Purley Oaks Primary School

THE GHOST HAIKU

The ghost was scary
The ghost vanished then came back
I was very scared.

Bobby Walker (11)
Purley Oaks Primary School

The Trip To The Loo

It's twelve o'clock midnight
I need to go, I am desperate.

I can't though, I really can't
. . . but I must.

I push back the duvet
The breeze tickles my toes
I place one foot on the floor, now the next,
Stand up
My knees are jelly
I walk over to the door
I switch on my torch
. . . *owwwwwwwww!*
I have just stepped on my sister's Lego.
I put my hand on my mouth
I have to carry on
My torch flashes on the bathroom door
I am here, I open the door
And sit on the loo . . . I have done it
I don't want to do it tomorrow night!

Vicky Gunner (10)
Purley Oaks Primary School

Lightning, Lightning

Lightning, lightning flashing down to the sea
Lightning, lightning, where could it be?
It went so fast that I couldn't see
Lightning, lightning, please go back to thee,
And never come back to me.

Ben Burke & Chevoy Johnson (9)
Purley Oaks Primary School

NORMAN MOLE

Norman Mole
Was an unfortunate soul.
His mum was quite mad
And thought he was bad.
He was made to eat string,
The poor little thing.
She also gave him worms,
To eat on all terms.
They wriggled in his stomach,
While being called a 'lazy lummock'.
The neighbours heard the noise
And clutched their little boys.
He was taken into care
And he loved it there.

But the worms started to hurt
Because they were coated in dirt.
It made him sick
And undoubtedly thick.
One night before six
He snapped three short sticks
Said 'I'm going to die,
Goodbye friends, goodbye.'
With his hands behind his head
He dropped down dead.

Katie Elliott (10)
Purley Oaks Primary School

Frankenstein Haikus

As Frankenstein lurks
Around the rundown building
Children are sleeping.

He walks very slow
And sends shivers down your spine
Leaving a bad smell.

It smells horrendous
And is in some kind of steam
It can make you faint.

His head is steaming
He is very angry now
You better watch out.

Conor Hack (11)
Purley Oaks Primary School

The Horror Within! Haiku

Deserted hallways,
With mad scientists lurking!
And floorboards creaking!

Deserted old house
Full with spooky old attics
Hear ghostly noises.

Eve Livesley (10)
Purley Oaks Primary School

THE SCIENTIST! HAIKU

The old scientist
His laugh echoes through the night
His glowing eyes gleam!

The full moon glows bright
Mad scientist out of sight
He fights the bad pain!

At the dead of night
The clock strikes twelve, *howl, howl, howl!*
The scientist stood.

Emma Grogan (10)
Purley Oaks Primary School

THE LOST DOG

I once had a lost dog
He just wandered off
He never came back
Because he was afraid
To get a smack.
He went to the shops and brought a pack of flapjacks.
He opened them up
And guess what he saw?
A card saying 'You have won a free trip abroad'.

Shivam Patel (9) & Bradley Talbot (10)
Purley Oaks Primary School

MY WISHES

I have wished many things
One was that I had a pet that sings.
Another wish was I was never depressed,
And everything was freely expressed!
Most of all that my brother was fat,
Very weak and hairy as a rat.

A very weird wish was that, there was a giant chocolate ball
Also that everyone would never fall.
I wish that my home was very large,
And over all of it I was in charge!
Some of the wishes have been very bad,
And a lot of them might seem very mad.

I wish I had a palace as big as can be,
And everyone from around the world would come to see.
I wish I were a king, but without a queen,
Because then I wouldn't be mean.
But I prefer to be a boy,
And play with all my lovely toys.

My wishes have been really great,
But I don't always get them straight.
I always wish a lot,
Once I wished for a magic pot.
Wishing is a lot of fun
And is the best thing I have done.

Arjoon Niranjan (9)
Reedham Park School

MY DREAM

In my dream I met a strange man,
With a long black beard and a purple hand.
He had yellow, bright eyes that shone like the sun,
And his long black hair stretched down his face.
His ears were small, his nose was red, his face was whiter
than the pillow of a bed.
His nails were long and brown like a berry,
His lips were the same colour as a cherry.
He wore sandals on his feet and his robes were long with
strange symbols neat.
His glasses were round and looked very new
He had a rod with a jewel at the end for he knew magic
like no other thing,
He conjured up a table with magnificent food,
And we talked about how beautiful the full moon was.

Manu Babu (9)
Reedham Park School

THE ZOO

I saw a baby hippo as it played in the water,
I saw a lion as it roared, and its cubs.
I saw a tiger as it was stalking its prey,
I saw a monkey as it played among the trees.
I saw an elephant as it ate the leaves,
I saw a crocodile as it swam in the water.
I saw a parrot and it was mimicking my words,
I saw a snake as it was slithering on the grass.
I saw a shark as it swam in the water,
I saw a cheetah as it ran in the field - and then -
I left and went home.

Aaron McGuigan (9)
Reedham Park School

Horses

I like horses very much,
They are kind and gentle,
They are also very beautiful,
I like the way they tickle me,
The movements are swift and sometimes
delicate.

I went riding one day
I was riding a lovely horse,
She was blonde so I called her Blondy
I do miss her so, for I do not know where she is,
I hope she is safe and with nice and kind people.

All the horses I have been on have been wonderful
They gallop so beautifully,
Their mane and skin are so soft,
They are graceful sometimes,
They are my favourite animals out of every animal
in the whole world.
I love horses and I always will do.

Hayley Bogaerts (9)
Reedham Park School

THE SEA

The raging, blazing devil
Gleaming in the sunlight,
People stop and stare,
Oh, what a beautiful sight.

Fish of all sizes
Are under that huge quilt,
Swimming ever so happily,
'Neath where the pier is built.

The sea is sometimes kind, like a nurse,
Letting children play,
In its waters where the sun
Is shining throughout the day.

The sea is sometimes fierce as a lion
Roaring louder and louder,
The waves are slashing at the shore
And the froth is like white powder.

When the day is over
Home the people go,
While the raging, blazing devil
Pulls the tide out low.

Nasha Raman (11)
Reedham Park School

THE STABLE

By the stable office I stand,
In my jods and riding hat,
I'm all alone, I gaze about me,
The smell of sweet hay wafts around;
I look at the ponies, they're ready now,
I mount Bella, the black mare,
And ride off.

I'm back from my ride,
Take off my black hat,
I bury my face in Bella's mane,
It smells of leather and straw,
I serve her lunch,
Sticky, sweet chaff covers my fingers,
I lick it.

Time for Bella to go up to the field,
I mount, my hat's on again,
No saddle, just a dusty green rug,
The wind whips my face,
It stings like an injection,
I tuck my chestnut hair behind my ear,
And ride up.

It's three o'clock,
Time to go
I'm sad,
I gather up my stuff,
Rucksack and grooming kit,
One last look around
And step reluctantly in the car.

Imogen Wainwright-Jones (9)
Reedham Park School

The Charmed Ones

There are three girls who are charmed,
They can never ever get harmed.
Their names are Prue, Phoebe and Piper,
Phoebe is always acting hyper.
The girls have to use the Book of Spells
They are always sending demons to Hell.

There was a demon called Cole,
Who the girls pushed into a black hole.
A white lighter called Cleo,
Often helped the trio.
When Phoebe was little she was looked after by nuns,
Now she is one of the charmed ones.

The eldest is Prue,
A good witch, through and through.
With the power of three, they do so well,
Together they work on many spells.
They use their magic only for good,
To use evil spells they never would.

Sister number three
Is Piper - you'll see
Her heart is good and true,
When helping Phoebe and Prue.
Piper sometimes feels fear,
Although not when her sisters are near.

Together the sisters fight,
Demons and creatures of the night.
For goodness and love always wins,
Against evilness and sins.
The sisters triumph you see,
For they have the power of three.

Faye Kearns (10)
Reedham Park School

The Fashion Show

I love fashion
It is my passion
My mum said, 'Go on Lucy.'
My nickname is Lucy Juicy.

I felt so tense
What I whispered made no sense.
The outfits were fantastic,
I felt like shouting, 'They're made from elastic.'

I felt so sad, the day was done,
I felt like I was number one.
I said to my friends, 'I'll see you soon.'
That was when I felt over the moon.

Lucy Mackenzie (10)
Reedham Park School

Maths

Oh! I do hate maths, sitting at the table for hours on end.
I stare out the window and watch cars go round the bend.

Algebra, geometry - do we have to measure?
Some people do maths for pleasure!

I loathe maths homework, add, subtract, multiply and divide.
I'd rather be in the garden on my slide.

Problem solving is very tricky,
And when I get it wrong people take the mickey.

Maths, maths, maths, that's all I get,
So good luck to my reader; your troubles of maths aren't over yet.

Marina Guy (11)
Reedham Park School

Sports Cars

A Ferrari is a car I've seen,
To buy one I am very keen.
I know they are a lot of money,
But you can drive them with
The roof down, when it's sunny.

I would show my friends my beautiful car,
And I would drive very, very far.
My dad once drove an Aston Martin,
And when he was young, he went go-karting.

Soon I hope I'm going to get a go-kart,
And I will go as fast as a dart.
I will race on a difficult track,
And leave everyone a long way back.

Oliver Ash (10)
Reedham Park School

I Wish I Was A Princess

If I was a princess I would stand very tall
And every night I would host a ball.
I would treat people equally, no one would be poor.
I'd name my country Moon Crystal.
I'd sit on my royal throne very proud
While everyone was singing loud.
Oh how I wish that a princess I could be
I would have a humungous garden
Oh so beautiful, oh so colourful
I would go out and ride my very own special pony.
Oh but this wish will never come true
Don't you wish you were a princess too?

Toni Akinajo (9)
Reedham Park School

My Precious Barbie

My precious Barbie has a lovely face
I wish she would come with me to space.
I play with her nearly every day,
I wish she could walk with me a little way.

Her hair is very long,
And when you press a button she sings a lovely song.

I washed and coloured her hair so fine,
I plaited her hair this took a long time.

She is such a lovely toy,
When I am with her she gives me so much joy.
She has prettiest of looks,
I like to read her all my books.

Temilade Oni (10)
Reedham Park School

The Lottery Dream

Keep all your hope for Wednesday nights.
For Mum is shouting 'Turn on the TV!'
And 'Switch on the lights.'
I hear my sister upstairs shout 'Oh! me! me! me!'

Get the ticket and sit right down.
Six of the numbers are right that means we've won!
I think the cheque would weigh a ton
Then for my birthday I'll have a clown.

Clash, bang, I woke with a fright
It was all a dream
And switch on the light
Oh the world can be so mean.

Jessica Sneddon (10)
Reedham Park School

My Family

When I'm with my mum and dad,
I feel so very very glad.
With my brothers it is different,
My mum said she meant,
To give me a sister,
But none of the babies she had were a 'her'.

My aunts and uncles are different by far,
I think they think my mum's bizarre,
For having so many of us,
My dad says we always want something
Like having a ride on a bus,
I don't think he means it about me,
Anyway I'm just glad we are one big family.

Joanna Parkins (9)
Reedham Park School

I Wish . . .

I wish I had a pet,
I would always take it to the vet.
My ideal pet would be a dog,
I would probably name him Tod or Tog.

I wish that I could fly,
And when I fall that I won't cry.
If I could, I'd fly to school,
Everybody would think I'm cool.

I wish that I could run a mile.
And swim along the River Nile.
I would win all the races,
And they'd be lots of angry faces.

Sonya Sivadasan (11)
Reedham Park School

SPIDERS

I really hate spiders,
It is the legs that I hate,
Well, they do have eight,
They are very creepy.
They are never very sleepy,
But when they are on their web
they look like gliders.

Spiders can have long legs, short legs,
or legs that are hairy,
Spiders can have small bodies, or big ones,
They might have some sons,
Well never mind about that; just never step on them,
Once a spider sat beside me and I had my elbow beside it.
I find spiders very scary.

Stephanie Lawden (10)
Reedham Park School

ANIMALS

Animals are sweet
Dogs give us wet feet
Some are vicious
Some taste delicious
You can keep some in a box
Just like a kitten, unlike a fox
Wolves hunt in packs
Unlike lazy cats sitting on mats
Just like a man riding a horse
Unlike a rabbit running a race.

Joel Schoburgh-Crooks (9)
Reedham Park School

In My Room

In my room it's full of gloom,
Almost like a tomb.
I have a closet eight feet tall,
And a cupboard, very small.
There is a train track with a train,
The train on the track even has a name.
My desk is all full of paper,
A pencil, pen and even an ink eraser.
I have some magazines all about trains,
And I have lots more all about planes.
My room is really, really messy,
I lost a cuddly toy called Tessy.
You really must see my room,
My room is full of gloom like a tomb.

Andrew Guest (8)
Reedham Park School

A Day Out

I went to bowling with my friends
I never wanted the fun to end
I went to bowling in a bus
I was very tired and made a big fuss.
My friends and I had to go
But I asked to stay and Mummy said 'No!'
We walked to the park in the breeze,
And saw the birds, leaves and trees.
My friend Jasonia pushed the swing,
And pushed it very high.
It felt like I was in the sky,
And that I could really fly.

Annabelle Ade-Jones (9)
Reedham Park School

How And Why

Are you always asking how or why?
Like why is blue the tint of the sky?
How come teachers get everything right,
And never get dirty when wearing all white?

Why are there so many stars in the sky,
And how is it that birds can fly?
Why is chocolate so tasty to eat,
And vegetables could never be so sweet?

Why is the beach always sunny,
But homework never so funny?
Why are secrets never told?
I wish one day they would just unfold.

Why is art so much fun,
When maths makes me feel so dumb?
How is snow so very cold?
You love it when you're young but not when old.

Why do people wander around at night?
The thought gives me quite a fright.
Why do people love the smell of a rose?
Because it's delicious I suppose.

Vicki Laffey (10)
Reedham Park School

My Teacher

She taught the children good and bad,
Her life was sometimes very sad.
There was always a smile on her face,
And she taught children how to tie a shoelace.

Her lips were always very glossy,
She was never known as a 'Miss Bossy'
One day we went to the park,
She was as happy as a lark.

When she got home she had no dinner,
Which made her look even thinner.
Next day when she entered class,
Everyone stared as she walked past.

To make her happy the children tried,
But it put her quite out of her stride.
The children said 'Sorry' for being naughty,
But it made her feel even more haughty.

Georgia Price (10)
Reedham Park School

MY CAT IS MY FRIEND

Animals are fun,
Sometimes I take mine out in the sun.
I play with mine all the time,
Sometimes they are boring,
Because they cannot speak a line.
Sometimes my cat is always in a mood,
Because it wants his food.
Each night he has to sleep outside,
But he never gives up his pride.

My cat is never scared
My sister never cares,
I love my cat because
He's cool, but it's too bad
He doesn't go to school.
My cat is always running with his friends,
He sometimes scares the chickens,
And the big fat hens.
When I'm asleep at night,
He sometimes gives me a really good fright.
Cats do not give you a scare,
Sometimes they might climb on your chair.
But please take care.

Clara-Louis McKrieth (8)
Reedham Park School

THE LAND OF FUN

It was great
I went there with a mate
Dolphins jumping through the air
I could not believe I was there.
Unicorns glistening bright
Their coats were lovely and white.

There were flying pigs,
Eating chocolate figs
The sun went down
We slowly walked into town.
Whizzing rockets went in the sky,
My friend and I said, 'Bye.'

I went into a ride
All the people began to hide.
Then it started to go round
I could not even feel the ground.
Then it became night,
And I went to catch my flight.

Rhia Sharma (11)
Reedham Park School

Hullabaloo

Hullabaloo, that's what I'm in
I could write about how I hurt my shin.
But that would be boring, and silly too
So instead of that, how about the zoo?

I'm staring out the window now
My teacher tells me to write but how?
I'd better think of something quick
How about when I was sick?

It isn't fair, that I can't write
I could tell how I gave my brother a fright.
I can't write a thing, even if I try,
I suppose it's better than telling a lie.

While I think about what my teacher said,
I realise I've said it all in my head.
All along I've been thinking of what to write,
I'll put it down now and hopefully I'll get it right.

Jessica Russell (11)
Reedham Park School

A Spaceman And An Alien

A spaceman zoomed off into space,
The fierce wind blowing in his face.
The green-headed alien laughed with joy,
Captain Bob was now a boy.
For he had travelled through a time machine,
Zonko the alien seemed very mean.
He cackled and laughed and his face was green,
He had a spotty ship like Bob had never seen.
He had googly eyes and a massive nose,
He also had seventeen toes.
His friends were pink with bright blue spots,
Captain Bob had seen aliens lots.
The alien invited him to dine,
Bob had such a very fine time.
Then he zoomed to his little flat,
To see his most adorable cat.

Lucy Doyle (10)
Reedham Park School

WHY?

Why are animals different?
Why not the same?
I wouldn't care if elephants
Had big fluffy manes!

Why do giraffes have spots?
Why not rosettes or stripes?
I wouldn't care if they had dots,
Or even smoked tobacco pipes!

Why do rabbits have fluffy tails?
Why not any at all?
I wouldn't care if they were blown off
in gales
Or even if they were small.

Why don't animals all come from Kent?
Why aren't they all tame?
Why are animals different?
Why not the same?

Abi McGilvray (10)
Reedham Park School

THE JUNGLE

In the jungle you find elephants,
And lots of bugs and ants
You might find a few warthogs
Or lions sleeping next to logs
They could eat a full-grown man.

In the jungle you would probably find a lake,
Animals bathe in it otherwise they might bake.
There are constrictors called boas
And probably some cobras.
Have you ever seen a real live snake?

In the jungle you find trees,
And probably some fleas.
Monkeys eat termites
And tigers have black stripes
They could eat you if they please.

Ellie Prior (9)
Reedham Park School

LIONS

Lions are fierce and brave,
They prowl about in a cave.

They run about at night,
And their eyes are very bright.

If they are too close in sight,
They might just take a *bite!*

They are very cute,
And they wear a brown, furry suit.

They have hard, sharp claws,
And the lioness, does most of the chores.

They lay down in the jungle as quiet as can be,
And they hunt for their prey as far as they can see.

If you run your legs get sore,
But not the lions, and they can *roar!*

Tharini Thirukkumar (9)
Reedham Park School

My Cat

My cat is not very fat,
Even though he eats a lot.
When he sees food, he's off like a shot!
Oh and about his hair - when he scratches, it's everywhere.
He fights with next-door's cat called Max,
If my cat Pip was human he would hit him with an axe.
To his bowl he is running
Sees a lady cat but no not very stunning.
Sometimes he just sits there laying in the sun,
And when we come back home from school he yawns
And stretches, as though he's done.
But wait, there is so much more,
He lies there on the floor,
Looking as though he is dead,
But really he is using the floor as his bed.
We have bought him a proper bed,
But no he likes the floor instead.
Pip chews my shoe but not my hat,
Never mind that I love my cat.

Andrew Russell (9)
Reedham Park School

THE WORLD

If the world was square,
You could not make it round,
This is life.

If the world was the sun,
You could not live on it,
This is life.

If the world was rectangular,
We'd fall off the edge!
This is life.

If the world was black,
We could not see each other.
This is life.

If the world was a clock,
Every second there would be an earthquake.
This is life.

Stephen Dowset (10)
Reedham Park School

World War III

It's not easy growing up in World War III,
Because you don't know what is going to happen
to your family,
Sometimes I feel really lonely,
Sometimes I feel terrified,
Sometimes I feel I'm going to die.

It's not easy to get shot,
It's not easy to die,
But when World War III is over,
You don't know if anyone is dead or alive.

It's not easy if relatives are dead,
It's not easy if I was dead,
But you just have to move on,
That is the way life is.
Some people say 'Let's go out and forget about it.'
I really miss my mum and dad,
But that is the way life is.

Ashleigh Hall (9)
Reedham Park School

My Mum And Dad

My mum and dad tell me off,
Even though I do not care,
My mum and dad send me to bed,
Then I feel so sad.

I sneak into my mum's cupboard,
I get told off for that.
In my house it gets so boring on my own.
Then I just go out.

I like to go on the computer,
But my mum is always on it.
I feel so sad,
I want to cry.

My dad is out,
My sister is out with her friends.
I feel so lonely with my family out,
I feel so lonely without my mum or dad.

James Hedges (10)
Reedham Park School

What I See

I see the birds and trees,
And all the buzzing bees.
I see the butterflies,
They are a lovely sight.

I see the pretty leaves,
Dancing in the air.
I see the lovely sky,
Passing by and by.

I see all the cows,
Going moo! *Moo!*
I see some horses
Sharing some fun,
Making noises for everyone.

I saw a big, big bear
Dancing everywhere,
The farmer is mowing the hay,
And is sitting in his tractor.

Ashleigh Blackwood (8)
Reedham Park School

WANTING A PET

I have always wanted a pet,
I'd always remember the day we first met,
We would play all day until we were tired,
If it were a dog I would take it for walks.
If it were a parrot I'd get one that talks,
But if I had a rabbit I'd feed it carrots daily.

Running down to the pet shop would be fun,
To get grams of pet food, maybe a tonne.
Days and days go by without the little friend I've always
wished for,
Something with a claw or a paw,
I'd be friends with it forever more.
We'd always be together,
I would make sure we were never separated.

I have loads of figures of animals,
With whom I am best pals,
I'd be even closer if I had a real one.

Berenice Graham (8)
Reedham Park School

My Dogs

Oliver and Chloe are pretty mad,
They are probably the maddest we've ever had.
They play all the time,
They are the family's and of course mine.

Ollie's a boy,
And Chloe's a girl.
I love it when they just stand there,
And both their tails curl.

They love their little walks,
They run around and around,
Sometimes to us Chloe talks,
And Oliver, us he found.

I love my dogs so so much,
I think I am so lucky,
To have dogs like them,
Even though they are sometimes mucky.

Marissa Beatty (8)
Reedham Park School

My Friend

My friend is my dog
We play ball
And we love each other.
She wakes me up
And licks me a lot.
I love my dog.

When I throw snowballs she licks them
And she is fluffy.
She chases the cats
And she is my friend
I love my dog.

My dog nicks my food
When I come home she wants a cuddle.
I give her biscuits every day
I want my dog when I'm at school
I miss my dog.

Jade Sherwill (8)
Reedham Park School

THE FAIRIES

Down the rushy glen,
The fairies are awake
By a big fat hen.
The children are out
The children fight,
The fairies say 'Get out of sight.'
The mums always shout,
'Get out!'

The frog has a golden pipe,
The cakes have turned to mould.
Every child is playing,
All the shops are making,
The Queen fairy is good,
And they have delicious food.
They always think
But they have lots to drink.

Marissa Nurse (8)
Reedham Park School

I Like

I like chocolate,
I like it when it melts in my mouth,
I like it when it's in tiny pieces,
I like it when it's boiling hot,
I like it when it's as cold as ice,
That's why chocolate is so nice.

I like crisps,
I like them because there's so many flavours,
I like them when they're cheesy,
I like them when they're salty,
I like them when they taste like onions.

I like sweets,
I like the different colours,
I like the ones with juice inside,
I like the ones that are chewy,
I like the ones that are gooey,
To be honest, I like everything.

Selexis Stephens (10)
Reedham Park School

MY DREAM PET

I have always wanted a pet,
Since I was four.
And saw one come through the door.
I saw a dog and then a cat,
Then a parrot and then a bat.
I asked my mum for a mouse,
But she said it would run through the house.
Mum asked me what was wrong,
Which was nice,
I said I would like some baby mice.
A week went away,
And still I waited,
But then I remembered it was my birthday.
My mum had a present for me with a surprise,
A pet in our lives.

Bronte Jack (8)
Reedham Park School

ROMANCE LOVE

Darling, your colour is a creamy pink,
Your sweet smell of a beautiful perfume.
Your sound makes me want to listen more and move to you.
You look like a beauty queen
And taste like a wonderful milkshake, a sugary milkshake.
You feel like a smooth rock.
So my dream has come true,
My beloved one, so I will always remember you.
I love you darling!

Yousif Mahdi (10)
Royal Kent CE Primary School

Love

Pink and passionate like a glider
Flying through the air gently and smooth.
Silken with passion
Strong and brave, not weak and frail.
Love is beauty and love is light
Not dark and ugly.
Smooth and calm is love
And the taste of passion fruit
Luscious tangy and dippy
With sweet juice
Like a cherry blossom
Blowing the breeze through the air
Like a hummingbird
Fluttering around and through a forest of care.
The feeling of safety
And love and life come together.

William Janes (10)
Royal Kent CE Primary School

Love

Is sweet,
Warm smooth love flowing through the air,
Warm smooth chocolate melting in the boiling sun.
With the kiss of love.
But sad when you're on your own.
Oh how I love thee.
The touch of your warm kiss.
Whenever I'm on my own I think of thee.
How kind, how sweet you are
For it was luck that got us together.

Otis Brayer (9)
Royal Kent CE Primary School

LOVE

The feel of soft, gentle fluff on your fingertips
Letting you relax,
And forget your worries.
Passion in your heart and soul.
Pink the colour of understanding and beauty.
Perfume invading your sense of smell.
Taste of hot chocolate sliding down your throat.
Loving every minute.
Joyful and colourful like a rainbow.
The sound of a youthful woman singing,
With all her soul, putting in all her determination
Creating perfection in your soul.

Katherine Yearley (10)
Royal Kent CE Primary School

SADNESS AND DEPRESSION

Sadness is black, full of depression.
Still like a tree
The taste of raw fish,
Running down your dark and gloomy throat,
A drink of Coke; black and cold
Like an explosion from the can.
The smell is like rice pudding;
Cold and runny,
It feels like a needle stabbing in your back.
The sound of a motorbike
Revving up its engine
Like a motorbike zooming into you.

Bethany Bradford (10)
Royal Kent CE Primary School

Love

Red is the colour of blood rising through hearts.
Red is the colour of lava, the colour of love.
Red raspberry chocolate,
Shapes of hearts
Taste lovely.
Fresh strawberry
In a bowl of love
Smell delicious.
The beaming heart in the sky
Like the sun on Valentine's Day.
Hearts beating and thumping
People munching chocolates,
Children singing and humming merrily
I feel excited wondering
If I'll get a Valentine's Card or not.

Rhys Davies (10)
Royal Kent CE Primary School

Depression

Depression is more than sorrow
It is much worse.
It is as black as death
And will not stop.
You are trapped in your own head
Drums faintly beating through your mind.
A growing darkness trying to engulf you,
You cannot hide.
It is approaching, slowly like a snake, slithering
To engulf us in darkness.
    The end is near.

Noah Granger (9)
Royal Kent CE Primary School

Love

Pink, colour of blossom blooming,
Calm and relaxing, joy spurting
Helping you breathe pure air.
Birds chirping their beautiful song,
Music, quiet and soft, passing overhead.
Smell the perfume, drifting above.
Blurriness surging towards you.
Absorbing it, falling into harmless sleep.
Taste the sweetness of passion fruit.
Its sugary goodness coursing through your veins.
The best thing you've ever tasted.
Touch smooth sand on the beach.
Feel the grain trickling through your delicate fingers.
See the waves, lap up at the edge of the sand,
And watch the foam bubble up.
Feel warm and fizzy inside,
Dazed but happy
Now, that is love.

Rowena Hill (10)
Royal Kent CE Primary School

Love In Spring

Pink like a new flower blooming in the sun.
The petals so smooth.
A newly baked cake,
That tastes so sweet.
The smell so great.
Love flowing down the river,
As it rushes down so fast.
The cute little bluetits singing their songs,
As all the trees are swaying in the breeze.
It feels like spring has just started.
But now it's all over.
Love tastes like strawberries in a golden dish,
Waiting to be eaten.
The wind like an owl,
The trees look like hands reaching out to grab you.
Love is here.

Emily Smith-Drane (10)
Royal Kent CE Primary School

FEAR

Black and cold on a slushy wet night,
Moonlight shining down on me
Laughing, laughing loudly.
The taste of bitterness trailing down my mouth.
Dark, cold alleyways,
Damp and freezing like a chill.
A quick breeze rushing past my face.
As you look in the dead of night,
Pale faces smile at you hiding secrets you don't know.
Screech! The sound of ghosts white like a blanket glowing in the night.
Echoing, an owl's hoot wakes up nightmares,
That creep in your mind silently.
Quietly ashes from a fire falling to the ground.
Slowly, slowly freezing air,
Panic, panic.
Fear is always near.

Amy Stewart (9)
Royal Kent CE Primary School

HATE

Hate.
A flaming hot red
And a fearful dark black.
Burning, burning,
Red-hot chilli peppers,
And a devil's head.
Burning, burning.
Always it retreats,
But the anger draws nearer.
Burning, burning,
Drilling a hole in your heart,
Of hatefulness.
Burning, burning,
It is not forgotten
But dies down as other things take its place.
Burning, burning
Do you ever feel like this?
Burning, burning
In your own world of hate.
Burning, burning
Away!

Victoria Millward (9)
Royal Kent CE Primary School

DEPRESSION

Black, burning hatred,
running through your boiling bloodstream,
racing rapidly
not flowing gently,
but painful,
anger with raging amounts,
of sorrow and madness.
Most of all is pure anger,
anger grows bigger, bigger.
More depressed,
and more depressed.
Then you're out of control.

Jealousy, sorrow, anger, disappointment.
Sadness, hatred, madness,
anxious, worried,
all fits into one big blazing uncontrollable
unstoppable
depression
and stress
also Hell is where you live
but you can't get away from it.

Chantelle Sayers (10)
Royal Kent CE Primary School

JEALOUSY

Envy rushing through my veins
Like blood but faster than anything.
Everything is bright green,
Turning everything all horrible.
So uncomfortable that I could scream,
The taste of metal swarms into my mouth,
Hatred running free into my brain
Buzzing like a thousand bees tickling my toes
Stinging me at every possible moment,
In every possible place,
Driving me mad,
Trying to play as cool as I can,
It's really hard.
A great big red-hot fire burning up my kindness,
Turning me as evil as evil itself.
Furious thoughts rule my head,
Hard to fight,
Hard to leave,
Jealousy too strong other people can see it,
That lonely feeling sweeps over me,
Any friends disappear,
Until I let it out,
I am done.

Elizabeth Springford (9)
Royal Kent CE Primary School

Love

Love as soft as the smooth calm breeze flowing through your hair.
Pine as soft as fresh green grass,
As soft as a baby's skin.
A majestic blossom floating through the thin atmosphere,
As soft as the sea slowly rising up onto your skin,
As you feel the rush of sand in-between your toes.
The taste of the smooth strawberries in your mouth moving
slowly down to your stomach.
The sight of the daffodils slowly, but calmly growing in the
soft tender soil.
The soft feeling of love inside your heart,
Pumping of your blood going round your body.
The sound of the birds tweeting in their trees.
The smell of freshly baked cakes being taken out of the oven.

Jonathan Berry (10)
Royal Kent CE Primary School

Mad

Red and rapid as a bonfire
As hot as a raging volcano
Swishing in and out like a tide.
Feels like someone has punched you round the face,
And the Devil has ripped out your soul.
Smells like an acid cloud of smoke.
The sight of it will strike fear into your heart.
It will burn your hand
Tastes like a flaming doughnut
That has just been put down your throat.
Burning in the pit of your belly
Sounds like something is scorching your ear
And thumping on your head.

Marcos Zakakiotis
Royal Kent CE Primary School

LOVE

The sight of the first flower blossom,
Calming yet magical,
As it waves in the air.
The smell of sweet-scented perfume,
Taking over your senses,
Like creamy chocolates.
Pink is the colour of love,
Like a bowl full of strawberries,
The sound of soft raindrops falling,
As they hit the smooth sail,
It becomes silent.
Feels like golden sand trickling through your fingers
Into a dream.
The taste of melted chocolate,
Dripping down your mouth,
Making you relax.

Gemma Skilton (9)
Royal Kent CE Primary School

LOVE

Red as a hot bonfire,
Boiling hard like a wave,
Flowing out of a river of passion,
As majestic as a blossoming tree,
Swaying in the cold breeze.
The taste of the juicy strawberries,
The smell of daffodils in the soil.
The sound of a dog barking in the garden.
The crispy roast chicken sizzling out of the oven.

Ben Thomas (10)
Royal Kent CE Primary School

Joy

Joy is the colour of flowers,
Flowering buds turning into flowers,
While blossoming tulips in the hot sun,
Hoping you feel welcome.

Taste the hot chocolate that runs down your throat
And warms you up.
Chocolate reaches your heart and spurts love into it,
Helping you feel welcome.

Salt from the sea waves lapping against the golden sand,
Sugar from delightful chocolate,
Majestic flowers making you sneeze with their generous pollen,
Forming a welcome.

Seeing bonny people and surprised birds,
Palm trees flowing with the wind on the wonderful golden sand,
With its inhabitants,
Making you feel welcome.

Hearing birds call out happy musical sounds,
People singing joyful songs,
Leaves crackling and drifting down to the ground below,
Making you feel welcome.

Feeling generous giving someone a present,
Sharing your love with another person,
Being hopeful that they will appreciate the present,
Feeling happy and excited,
Creating a glorious welcome.

Eleanor Hutchings (9)
Royal Kent CE Primary School

Love

Red is the colour of love,
With hearts all around.
Big red sweet cakes
With juicy cherries on top.

Red is the colour of love,
With tulips opening and blossom blooming.
The wind bristling
Flowers shooting
Leaves blowing round.

Red is the colour of love
Inside the fire is blazing,
With big bright flames,
And little sparks flying.

Eleanor Singer (9)
Royal Kent CE Primary School

Snow

Thick layers of fluffy white snow falling to the ground,
We used to hear so many things, but now there is no sound.
Wrap up warmly; gloves, scarf and hat,
Looking at the dog sitting by the fire on a mat.
I love to make a snowman with a carrot as a nose,
With buttoned eyes and a beaded mouth in rows after rows.
Snow on the roof, a magical sight,
Children having a snowball fight.
I love it when it snows,
And I hope it never goes.

Emily Bacon (10)
St David's School, Purley

The Rainstick

The rainstick is an instrument made from wood and beads.
The wood came from the rainforest trees.
The rainstick is made by man to be played in a band
Accompanied by the maracas they make the sound of a
Tropical carnival.

The rainstick reminds me of a waterfall
As the water crashes down like a bucket in a well.
The beads remind me of dolphins in the sea as they shake
and jump about.

The rainstick sounds like small streamlets forming a tide at
the seaside.
The beads remind me of water running down like a tap
Being turned on and off then out comes clear blue water
rushing around.

Ryan Reid (10)
St David's School, Purley

Rainstick

R ain, hitting the muddy ground
A snake slithers around and around
I cy sheets cover the forest floor
N oises of rattling - even more
S wishing through the moonlight air
T ense silence everywhere
I magine a typical forest scene
C aterpillars, badgers it's just serene
K estrels flying through the trees
S ends along a chill breeze.

Joseph Rifaat (10)
St David's School, Purley

I WISH I WAS . . .

I wish I was a green, shiny alien flying in a flashing UFO.
I wish I was a tall, rocky volcano blowing up in a cloud of orange fire.
I wish I was a sleek, white spacerocket powering up from a smoky launchpad.
I wish I was a tense, strong cable holding up a grand suspension bridge.
I wish I was a very poisonous injection digging deep into soft skin.
I wish I was a giant, 100m tall waterfall cascading over the edge of a giant canyon.
I wish I was a fast, turbo-charged Porsche, hurtling down a fast lane.
I wish I was a stubborn, humpy camel, trekking over a dusty desert.
I wish I was a diving, bubbling submarine plummeting into the blue ocean.

How I wish!

Matthew Watson (9)
St David's School, Purley

THE ELEPHANT

The elephant is as grey as a mouse,
He is as big as a house,
With ears that flap around,
And a trunk that can touch the ground.

Strong, gentle and kind,
A more intelligent animal would be hard to find.
With eyes that look so sad,
We could never think of him as bad.

He walks very carefully,
Picks up logs very daringly,
With tusks as white as snow,
There is no other animal like him,
I know.

Olivia Rogers (9)
St David's School, Purley

Snow

Everything covered in a thick sheet of white,
Goodness me, what a sight!
I wrap up tightly in coats galore
The cold makes my toes sore.
All I can see is crystalled trees.
I wonder if snow covers the seas!
I find it hard to build a snowman,
But I tell myself I can!
We all start snowball fights.
It is not the time to fly kites.
Individual snowflakes fall down,
At this time no one wears a frown.
All I can hear, in fact there's nothing
Especially not any huffing.
In the end people hide,
I, just glide!

Becky Smith (11)
St David's School, Purley

The Rainstick

The rainstick, it has many holes through,
At first I thought it was a didgeridoo.
It's from Chile, South America.
But then again it sounds like my old harmonica.

It looks like a big hunk of wood,
I'd play it like an instrument if I could.
If you tip it over it makes a lovely sound,
Like many bees buzzing around
And rain falling on the ground.

Jay Patel (10)
St David's School, Purley

RAINSTICK

I am a rainstick
I am held proud and high
Rain is badly needed,
They point me to the sky.

I twist,
I turn,
And words are said aloud
Rain is badly needed,
Will I produce a cloud?

I want to help
I really do.
They made me with such kindness,
And I am trusted too.

So will I help my people
To grow their grain and seed?
I need the rain as much as them,
To give them all they need.

Rachael Sanders (11)
St David's School, Purley

THE RAINSTICK

The rainstick is an onomatopoeic sound
The swishing sound is very soft and soothing.

The rainstick makes me feel like I am cascading
Through white water rapids.

The rainstick sounds like the dripping of a tap
Or maracas.

Adam Bowley (10)
St David's School, Purley

RAINSTICK

Rainstick!
It sounds like . . .
The rattle of the rattlesnake,
The gurgling in the drain,
The rippling in the turquoise lake,
The patter of the rain.

It looks like . . .
The branches of the rowan tree,
The ancient didgeridoo,
The antennae of the bumblebee
The trunk of the palm tree too.

And I think it . . .
Is very soothing to your brain,
And very relaxing too,
It sounds refreshing like the rain,
And pleasant for me and you.

Olayinka Lauson (11)
St David's School, Purley

The Rainstick

The rainstick sounds like a waterfall,
Sounds like the rain it is trying to call,
Sometimes it sounds like a stream trickling,
Like lots of people bickering.

The rainstick sounds like a rainforest,
Where everything is nice and moist,
The sound is very soothing,
Like a stream when it is moving.

The rainstick sounds like pouring rain,
Trickling down the drain,
I think the sound is wonderful,
And it also looks delightful.

Sarah Dixon (11)
St David's School, Purley

The Panda

The panda is a gentle bear,
He climbs to the top of the tree and sniffs the air.
His favourite meal is bamboo shoots,
From this perch he can hear lots of animals hoot.

The panda is shy,
I don't know why.
With his beautiful black and white fur,
His appearance will always cause a stir.

This gentle creature is very rare,
It is most important that we all care.
If we lose this beautiful animal today,
Future generations will miss out in a very sad way.

Annabel Rathbone (9)
St David's School, Purley

Rainstick

It sounds like rain,
Running down a drain.
It has shingle inside,
Spreading far and wide.

It's like a pan sizzling,
Sometimes sounds like rain drizzling.
The stones go down the stick,
Like a flame down a wick.

It's made out of hollow wood,
And it makes the sound it should.
It sounds like rain on pebbles,
Or the chinking of medals.

Needles are pushed into the stick.
The shingle will be down in a tick.
The sound is relaxing,
Nothing else seems taxing.

Daniel Ashby (10)
St David's School, Purley

Animal Poem

Cheetahs live in dry places,
Cheetahs always play in races.
Cheetahs sleep in packs and pairs.
Cheetahs have a coat of hair.
Cheetahs know how to share,
Cheetahs leap in the air.
Cheetahs are as fast as lightning.
Cheetahs so very frightening.
Never seen at the speed of lightning.

Thomas Tawse (9)
St David's School, Purley

A Dog

Amber eyes
Staring at me
Begging for company.

Jumps
Runs happily
Licks my hand.

Play with me
Throw my toys
I will bring them back.

Go for a walk
Go for a play
Excitement.

Have a good time.

Nuala Armstrong-Walsh (9)
St David's School, Purley

The Polar Bear

Polar bears' fur is as white as snow,
In the dark it begins to glow,
They know when hunters come, so they go.

They play with their friends,
Till daylight ends,
Then return to their home.
Glad they are not alone
And snuggle up to their mother,
Like there is no other.

Abigail Wilson (10)
St David's School, Purley

The Penguin And Hamster

The penguin and the hamster
Are different animals you see,
They come from different places,
They are nothing like me!

The penguin looks like TV in the past
It smells of sea and fish,
It feels very smooth,
The penguin is like a wish!

The hamster looks like a blob of colour,
It smells warm and musty,
It feels furry and warm,
Its cage is very rusty!

The penguin and the hamster,
Are different animals you see,
They come from different places,
They are nothing like me!

Rhiannon Cogbill (9)
St David's School, Purley

Colours Of The World

Blue is the clear sky.
White is for the living.
Purple wonders why?
Pink is for the giving.
Black is death, that dead.
Gold and yellow have no mind.
Green is for the people who use their heads.
Still silver is for the kind.

Katie Staines (9)
St Martin's CE Junior School, Epsom

The Midnight Cry

I heard it at midnight,
At the crack of dawn, midnight.
Standing there, on the chair,
Was a cry coming from the sky.

But on the next day
I heard it again,
Was it a cry, was it a sin or was it a
Scale off a fish's fin?

I didn't know,
But on that night
I heard it once more.
But this time it was at the door,
It was knocking like madness,
Or was it just the sadness,
I didn't know,
And I'll never know.

Madeleine Cole (11)
St Martin's CE Junior School, Epsom

Barking Mad

I had a little dog
I think he's barking mad
I would not say he's never good
But most of the time he's bad.

He likes to play and he likes to run
And he likes to steal my toys
And when he has a rattly thing,
He makes a lot of noise!

Gemma Drewitt (11)
St Martin's CE Junior School, Epsom

There Is A Land

There is a land, a land where pink frogs skip round mulberry bushes.
A land where spotty gold goblins climb yellow beanstalks.

There is a land, a land where green penguins dance in the desert.
A land where purple ants do roly-polys on sheep.

There is a land, a land where orange rabbits eat green sandwiches.
A land where spotty jellyfish play cards.

There is a land, a land where witches munch blue honeycombs.
A land where purple tigers play hopscotch.

There is a land, a land where scarlet horses play hide and seek.
A land where violet butterflies gobble pink bananas.

There is a land, a land where stripy guinea pigs play snooker.
A land where all poems have to end.

Fiona Middleton (9)
St Martin's CE Junior School, Epsom

The Witches

We are witches of Hallowe'en ooh-hoo!
Our faces are crooked and green ooh-hoo!
We fly around at night
And give you such a fright!
We are witches of Hallowe'en ooh-hoo!

We carry our cats on our brooms ooh-hoo!
We scare kids asleep in their bedrooms ooh-hoo!
You might try to run away
But we'll come back another day
And our cats will still be on our brooms ooh-hoo!

Amani Salam (8)
St Martin's CE Junior School, Epsom

THE IMPORTANCE OF FRIENDS

My friends are so important to me,
It's more than just coming round for tea.
We sing and laugh and dance and play,
Sadly we can't do it every day.

Sometimes we don't see eye to eye,
And we often have been known to cry,
But making up is soon decided,
And again our secrets are confided.

A sleepover is such great fun,
A midnight feast for everyone,
But tired eyes remain the next day,
To do our homework not to play.

But our schooldays will soon be gone,
A distant memory or words to a song
Will bring the past all flooding back
Of a friendship that never turned its back.

Hannah Foxley (9)
St Martin's CE Junior School, Epsom

RAINBOW

Beautiful colours in a rainbow,
Red, orange, green and indigo.
Rain mixing with the sun,
Everybody is having fun.
Shining gold in a pot,
Find it if you're lucky,
Don't be sad if not!

Jessica Chinchen (8)
St Martin's CE Junior School, Epsom

Ants In Your Pants!

My dad said,
I had ants in my pants,
(and I wriggled).

My mum said,
'I'll give you a hand'
(I added it to my wrist).

My brother said,
'I have to keep an eye on you,'
(I better keep on rolling).

My uncle's jokes,
Drive me round the bend
(I ran back).

My grandma told me,
'To keep your hair on'
(I don't have any, I'm bald).

The farmer shouted
'The cows are coming home'
(I really must go).

My auntie said
'It's raining cats and dogs'
(Finally I get a pet dog).

My dad said
I had ants in my pants
(and I wriggled).

Nicola Boult (10)
St Martin's CE Junior School, Epsom

Fox Dinner!

Along the grass an animal sneaks,
There is no word he speaks,
Until he catches his prey,
Which would make his day!

Position is vital,
To keep his title,
Eyes staring,
Paws daring.

His timing has to be right,
He hopes to keep the daylight,
He keeps his confidence alive,
He has to catch to survive.

He pounces roaring,
Frightens the rabbit gnawing,
He finds his appetite,
And kills with one bite.

He pulls the dead rabbit,
Which has the gnawing habit,
Deep into his den,
For his cubs and vixen.

Eluned Broom (10)
St Martin's CE Junior School, Epsom

What Has Happened In The World Today?

What has happened in the world today?
Something terrible I can say!
It could be a *monster*
It could be a *bear!*
Whatever it is you better beware!

What has happened in the world today?
A rocket took off from its launching bay!
Did it *fire?*
Or did it *explode?*
Whatever it did it had a big load!

What has happened in the world today?
A bomb went off that's all I can say!
Was it *big?*
Or was it *small?*
I can tell you something it wasn't tall!

What has happened in the world today?
Nothing now I am sorry to say!
But we will be *back*
With more to *say!*
But that's what's happened in the world today!

Jeremy Hunt (7)
St Martin's CE Junior School, Epsom

My Cousin's In The Army!

My cousin's in the army,
He's going off to war,
I don't really understand,
What this war is for.

My cousin's in the army,
It's going to be hot,
I really hope he doesn't
Get himself shot.

My cousin's in the army,
I am feeling quite sad,
It makes me wonder,
Has everyone gone mad!

Katie Sevenoaks (10)
St Martin's CE Junior School, Epsom

Horses

Horses come in many sizes,
In the races they win prizes.
They sleep on shavings or on straw,
And they eat food that is raw.
Riding horses is sometimes fun,
You can go hunting on the run.
To muck out stables you need a spade,
Also horses need a lot of shade.

Horses need tack to ride,
When they're being ridden they stride.
When they go in their stable,
They eat from a bucket not from a table!

Tessa Derry (9)
St Martin's CE Junior School, Epsom

TITANS OF STEAM

(Based on 'Piggo's Train Ride' by Pam Ayres)

He's in the station,
Right in the nation
Boarding a train,
For Manchester Lane.

Mustn't be late, mustn't be late,
Mustn't be making the passengers wait.
Coal in the fire, smoke in the funnel,
Over the bridge and into the tunnel.

The train picks up speed,
With the coal all in need.
Smoke billowing out,
And spreading about.

With smoke and with fire,
People stand and admire.
As the train rattles by,
They wave it goodbye.

The train darts past
Here the junction comes
We've reached our destination
And civilisation at last.

Christopher Duncan (10)
St Martin's CE Junior School, Epsom

The Pine Marten

White fangs, bushy tail
Slitted eyes, sharp claws.
Thick fur to protect
From wind, snow and hail.

The winter skies are cold and grey
As padding quietly he walks
Always careful and alert
Whiskers twitching as he smells his prey.

A rabbit hops along the forest floor
As birds forage in the leaves
As the marten pounces
The birds fly off with great uproar.

Triumphant he drags it back to his nest
And feasts to his heart's desire
And after that he gets a drink
Then lies back to have a rest.

The pine marten is a predator fierce and savage
With killer fangs and claws
Woe to the creature that stands in its way
For with its insatiable appetite it will rip and ravage.

Emma Woolgar (9)
St Martin's CE Junior School, Epsom

PETS

Birds are going *tweet, tweet, tweet*
Lions and tigers are stamping their feet
Frogs are now the same colour as you
Mice are going *squeak, squeak, squeak*
Has something gone wrong?
Hullabaloo!

Cows are going *moo, moo, moo*
Cockerels are shouting *cock-a-doodle-doo*
Chicks are now the colour blue
Sheep are going *baa, baa, baa*
Has something gone wrong?
Hullabaloo!

Horses are going *neigh, neigh, neigh*
The scruffling sound of ponies eating hay
Squirrels will now never need the loo
Pigs are going *oink, oink, oink*
Has something gone wrong?
Hullabaloo!

Now you see some different pets
But then it's your decision which one you get.

Jodie Rogers (8)
St Martin's CE Junior School, Epsom

My Mum!

She's a warm bouncy bed,
She's an old, cuddly cat,
A sweet-smelling iris,
And a busy, buzzy bee.
She's a wise owl floating through the air,
A robin making its nest.

She's a rainbow-coloured diamond shining,
The sound of the orchestra,
A summer's evening with a relaxing, welcoming sunset,
She's a fizzy lemonade drink,
As loud as an elephant trumpeting,
But as quiet as a stingray.

She's as calm as a turtle,
A twisty maze to the centre,
A pretty young ballet dancer
She's a flexible jumpy gymnast
A brick wall when angry
A fun, bubbly Aero.

She's a tricky puzzle
A musical piano,
A lighted Christmas tree,
As magical as a witch,
A burning candle,
And she's my mummy!

Emily Runson (9)
St Martin's CE Junior School, Epsom

THE WRITER OF THIS POEM

(Based on 'The Writer Of This Poem' by Roger McGough)

The writer of this poem is . . .
as nice as can be
as strong as an athlete
as gentle as a tree.

As fast as a cheetah
as slow as a tortoise
as noisy as a baby
as silly as a porpoise.

As mad as her dad,
as daft as a deer,
as cool as a pop star,
and she's as sharp as a spear.

Rebecca Green (9)
St Martin's CE Junior School, Epsom

SUMMER'S BREEZE

In among the summer's breeze,
The dancing flowers and the trees.
In an overgrown patch a bramble bush grows,
Scratching skin and tearing clothes.
'Cut it down!' the birds have said,
'Cut it down it will be dead.'
So the rabbits worked and cut it down,
The children dig in the mud of brown.
In the garden life again,
The foxes live together in a cosy den.
Friendship between the animals,
Knocked down lay the barriers and the walls.

Emma Brooker (10)
St Martin's CE Junior School, Epsom

FRIENDSHIPS!

Life without friends
would be no fun at all,
if they are big,
or even small.

You can be friends forever,
or as much as a day,
you may play a game,
or have something to say!

Whatever it is,
a friend is so great,
I hope when I meet them
they won't be late!

Holly Soodhoo (10)
St Martin's CE Junior School, Epsom

THE EAGLE

The eagle is a bird,
Who swoops down to its prey,
To feed his wife and little ones,
At the end of every day.

The eagle is a wondrous bird,
It looks so golden and sly,
When it talks to its prey,
It squawks the word, '*Die!*'

But when this bird grows old,
It will die strong and true,
And all its helpful nature,
Will be gone because of you.

Keshini Jayawardana (9)
St Martin's CE Junior School, Epsom

The Midnight Man

I hear a creak down the hall,
I see a shadow across the wall,
I feel a hand touch my face,
Down the stairs I will race.

I see a door slowly close,
A funny feeling fills my toes.
I see a hand in the mirror,
Down my back I feel a shiver.

I feel a hand on my back,
Do I dare look back,
I hear a smash of a door,
Something scampers across the floor.

Sweat flows down my cheek,
I hear an enormous *creeeeeaak!*
My face shines from the moon,
Waiting what will happen soon . . .

Andrew Taylor (9)
St Martin's CE Junior School, Epsom

Winter Haiku

Raindrops are falling,
Pattering on the windows,
As the winter comes.

Frost freezes the drops,
Turning the world gleaming white,
With bright shining snow.

Sonal Patel (11)
Sanderstead Junior School

Snow, Snow

Snow, snow, why do you have to melt?
Why can't you stay here forever?
Everybody likes you, white snow when you come down
Snow, you are silent, you are silent.
Coming to the ground
And the houses are covered with snow.
The trees are not green anymore
So soft like cotton wool.
And nice and deep . . .
The children long to play outside.

Darren Emmanuel (10)
Sanderstead Junior School

A Cold Night

It was a cold night
Wind blowing on trees
People walking the cold streets.

Anay Patel (9)
Sanderstead Junior School

Winter Night Haiku

A long freezing night,
Weak bird dies, from cold and frost,
Moon sheds raindrop tears.

Haruka Mukai (11)
Sanderstead Junior School

Sunshine

Sunshine, sunshine,
Shine on me
We love the way you glow,
Glorious as can be.

We know when you come
And know when you go
We don't want to see the sun go
Sun, we beg you don't go.

Now the sun is going away
We don't want to see it go.
We pray and pray to make it stay
But nothing comes our way.

Then one night
The children woke up,
And went outside to play
Then the sun was there again
And it was there to stay.

Isidahome Aligbe (10)
Sanderstead Junior School

Snowflakes

Slowly drifting down,
Snowflakes blanketing the ground,
Make children happy!

Ayumah Asigri (11)
Sanderstead Junior School

FROST

Frost is an artist, she paints with a brush,
She paints on your window, she paints in a rush.
Frost paints with snow and ice,
Her pictures are gorgeously nice,
Frost paints fish, islands and ships,
And young girls with lovely blue lips!

Frost wears the night sky as her dress,
And the stars she wears, never grow less.
Her hair is long and inky-black,
Her skin is as soft as a velvet sack.
Her limbs are slim and pearly-white,
Her feathery wings give her the power of flight!

But when the sun rises, Frost must take flight!
She cannot bear the sun,
It is not for her, daylight's fun.

Siân Williams (9)
Sanderstead Junior School

A WINTER'S NIGHT HAIKU

Snow is coming down,
Slowly, slowly from the sky,
Making the world white.

Beautiful white street,
But no one is walking now,
On perfect icing.

In the hillside wood,
A tired fox hungrily,
Hopefully searching.

Shin Nakamae (10)
Sanderstead Junior School

A WINTER DAY HAIKU

I wake up to find
Snowflakes drifting from the sky,
They lay on the road.

They lay on the roof,
It's such a beautiful sight,
Everything is white.

Children love the snow
Making snowmen, fingers burn,
Hoping it won't go.

Alice Warrington (11)
Sanderstead Junior School

SNOWING NIGHT

Cold, freezing night,
The snow started to fall,
As night began.

Moon is rising up,
Showing her face,
Behind the grey clouds.

Snow is gliding down
The white snow covering the street
Painting the town white.

Natsuko Mukai (9)
Sanderstead Junior School

SNOWY DAY

'Snow, snow, come down,' the children are shouting,
'The world is coloured in white,
In the garden there is a snowman.
Here snowman wear my hat, wear my scarf,
You're my friend, please don't go.'

The adults wish there wasn't snow,
Snow don't be slippery,
Go into my mouth and melt,
Cars crash, cars smash,
The cars no longer move.

Cats toasting their toes,
Hiding from the snowy cold,
Weary of winter,
Dogs running around,
Leaving pawprints wherever they go.

The chimney's smoke from fires below,
The house is warmer now,
The children run inside to put their hand near the stove,
Everything is cold and dark outside,
But they are safe and warm . . .
    Tomorrow they will make snowballs.

Mariko Tanaka (10)
Sanderstead Junior School

COLDNESS HAIKU

A freezing cold night,
Ice-cold squirrels sheltering,
Tucked up in their beds.

Liam Sanders (9)
Sanderstead Junior School

Outside Looking In

Outside looking in I see . . .
Christmas lights lit up.
Children opening their presents with delight
As their faces turn into huge, happy smiles.
Mum is cooking Christmas dinner while the children
Happily play with their toys.
Dad is taking a photo of the children with their new presents.

I smell . . .
The roast turkey being cooked in the oven.
The smoke coming out of the chimney from the
Fire blazing inside.

I hear . . .
The fire crackling,
Paper tearing while Mum clears it up.
Laughing and screaming from the children as they
Get the presents they always wanted.

Natalie Cummins (9)
Stamford Green Primary School

Train

People sleeping peacefully
People peeping over the driver's seat
Dashing on the track
Under bridges
On bridges
Everybody's squeezed on the underground.

Christina Low (8)
Stamford Green Primary School

A Christmas Poem

Outside looking in I see . . .
Mince pies on a plate steaming.
The Christmas pudding's flames flickering.
Christmas cards displayed on the mantelpiece.
Different colours surround you.
Christmas trees lights glowing as bright as
Stars in the moonlight.
Families, Mum cooking roast dinner.
Dad drinking a bottle of beer.
Children watching Dead Ringers'.
Outside looking in I smell . . .
The fire crackling in the grate,
The smell of burning wood wafts out.
The roast dinner and all the trimmings
Float around me in the air.
My mouth waters.
The melting of the candles as the last one is lit.
Outside looking in I hear . . .
Crackers going *pop, bang* and *crack*
And the laughing of the children.

Catherine Walsh (9)
Stamford Green Primary School

The Underground

On the London Underground
People hurtling behind the yellow line
Doors opening and closing
People squashed and grumbling in their seats.

Alex Willcocks (8)
Stamford Green Primary School

Jack Frost

He creeps across the flowers
He creeps across the leaves
He creeps across the bushes
And the bark of all the trees.

Even if you call him he won't come inside
In fact if you call him he'll just run and hide.

He creeps across the flowers
He creeps across the leaves
He creeps across the bushes
And the bark of all the trees.

He's lighter than snow, sleet and rain
And once he visited you he will come again.

He creeps across the flowers
He creeps across the leaves
He creeps across the bushes
And the bark of all the trees.

Imogen Corbett (11)
Stamford Green Primary School

The Train

The train roars in like a lion ripping up a zebra,
People rushing here and there,
Inside I'm getting more jammed every minute,
The guard's face almost bursts as he blows on the whistle,
Okay here we go slow but getting faster,
It's getting louder,
Now we are hurtling past lovely views.

Amy McCormack (8)
Stamford Green Primary School

The Underground

The old cold station cramped with people,
You may hear the chime from the steeple,
It's hot and stuffy,
Some people may have a coffee.

A lot of people getting cross,
Their children picking at the moss
The hour has come, oh no!
Quick let's get out of here!

Emily Breese (8)
Stamford Green Primary School

The Underground

People rushing like panthers trying to catch their prey.
The train flies like a bird landing in the hay
The people squeezing through the doors just like squashed worms.
I'm on the floor shocked and scared like skeletons eating worms.

Eleanor Williams (8)
Stamford Green Primary School

Snowflakes

Snowflakes
Magical crystals,
Whirling and swirling,
Wonderful white diamonds,
Slushy, crunchy, mushy,
Calling me to play in the
Snow.

Griffin Leeds (10)
TASIS The American School In England

SNOWMAN

Today was a snow day,
Much to our delight,
We built a great big snowman,
And had a snowball fight.

First we rolled a big snowball,
For the snowman's middle,
A small one for the snowman's head,
They fitted together like a well thought-out riddle.

We stuck a carrot for its nose,
And coal for its eyes,
Two sticks with mittens for his arms,
And a scarf that was twice his size.

We put a fluffy blue hat on him,
And three buttons made of lead,
I asked my brother what to call him,
'Frosty Fred,' he said.

Mary Buswell (10)
TASIS The American School In England

Dream

I was dreaming a dream,
Of a fantasy land,
When a monster appeared out of nowhere,
It pushed me,
And I fell through the bits and bobs,
And pieces of dreamland,
Then I fell to the ground,
With a very loud scream,
That woke my mum, my dad, sister and brother,
Woke the neighbours, the town and even the major,
I jumped up off the floor,
And ran around screaming,
Like a mad wild horse.
I never dreamed that dream again,
But I still remember the wonderful fantasy land,
And the horrible monster,
Who spoiled my dream.

Kathleen Jump (11)
TASIS The American School In England

SLEEP

Have you heard of this thing called sleep?
You never cry,
You never weep,
But if you cry,
If you weep,
It doesn't matter because you're asleep.
There are many words for this wonderful thing,
Like nap, doze,
Snooze and repose,
But the easiest words to say are,
Hit the sack,
Hit the hay,
Every night at half past nine,
You take a reprieve from the sunshine,
You have dreams in sleep,
Of wonderful lands,
Lands of magic,
Lands of sands,
But you also have nightmares in your sleep,
Of monsters,
Vampires,
And red-eyed sheep,
This is what they used to say,
When the day has gone,
And the night will stay,
Night night,
Sleep tight,
Mind the bed bugs don't bite.

Philippe O'Connor (10)
TASIS The American School In England

Snow

The snow is slender and white,
It's like a blanket wrapped around you,
You feel so excited and grateful,
For it is so quiet and beautiful.

You want to stay there forever,
But you know that time goes by,
You're full of wishes and joy,
And you don't want to say goodbye.

You wish and wish a lot,
You think of the snow,
But now it's time to say goodbye,
So you walk,
    and walk
        and walk.

Katerina Kaczmarski (11)
TASIS The American School In England

A Winter Day To Remember

A winter day to remember
Is a time for family and friends

A winter day to remember
Is a day that never ends

Hot cocoa going down your throat
Oh how good it feels

A winter day to remember
Is with snow that never melts

A winter day to remember
Is a day with someone else.

Charlotte Cushing (9)
TASIS The American School In England

A FEELING YOU'LL NEVER KNOW

The cat's footprints are in the snow, he is trying to catch a mouse.
'What is this?' he says and runs straight into the house.
For many hours he licks his paws trying to keep them warm,
But little does he know he's brought in snow and his master isn't
pleased.

'What is this?' the master cries.
'Please, oh please, oh please,' said the cat.

The master is such a mean old man, trying to live good,
Very, very mean old man that always wears a hood.
'Out you go you stupid cat, trying to soil my floor,
Out you go you stupid cat, just outside my door.'

Poor old cat, cold and thin, just outside the door.
'I like the floor inside the door, oh I feel so poor.
A feeling you shall never know, poor old me, poor old me,
I hate snow.'

Thurston Smalley (10)
TASIS The American School In England

CREATION

Creation is when . . .

A field of tulips bloom in a rainbow of colours,
A tiny chick hatches from a fragile, white egg.

When the sun rises into the morning sky in pinks and purples,
And a rainbow spills out after the rain has disappeared.

Like a friendship anew and interesting,
Like a freshly scattered blanket of snow.

The song of a dove in the morning,
And a story ready to unfold.

Katlin Bole (10)
TASIS The American School In England

THE SNOWBALL FIGHT

The fight started the 25th of December
It is the fight that I'll remember.

It started when I hit my friend
I thought this fight would never end.

Then my sister joined the fight
And I aimed at her just right.

Then my sister's friends started to play.
She pushed me over
And in the snow I lay
I'll never forget this snow fight today.

Emily Goode (10)
TASIS The American School In England

WAIT

Time goes by in years to come,
People can be happy, sad or glum,
You sit there, you pause, you think, you wait,
Not a care in the world,
Just your fate.
Will I be happy? Will I be sad?
Will I be confused? Will I be glad?
No one knows,
Not a soul . . .
Not a being,
Not even me.

Karina Zetterberg (11)
TASIS The American School In England

Thanks

Thanks for the whistling of the trees,
Thanks for the dancing of the leaves,
Thanks for towers standing tall,
Thanks for babies that soon will crawl,
Thanks for the sun, nature and birds,
Thanks for writing, letters and words,
Thanks for lakes, seas and oceans,
Thanks for cream, medicine and lotions,
Thanks for thunder, lightning and rain,
Thanks for sorrow, healing and pain,
Thanks for running, jumping and laughter,
Thanks for happy ever and after.

Emily Churchill (9)
TASIS The American School In England

Snow Day

As I look out my window to this winter night
Snowflakes fall delicately as pieces of a puzzle fit perfectly.
This seasonal puzzle pieces together slowly.
These tiny particles travel swiftly to their own place.
Until they are in their impeccable formation.

When I wake in the morning it has completed its form,
It has covered every roof, bordered every window,
Crystallised every tree and has frosted the ground.

Children come outside to play in this snow-blanketed land,
The snow clumps together as they leave footprints in the weather,
That's my snow day.

Camila Aguais (10)
TASIS The American School In England

WINTER WONDERLAND

Winter is wonderful and colourful.
It's as white as a turtledove, as dull as a pole, and
full of white snow.

Full of kids hustling and bustling
to win a fight -
now that's 'all right!'
To get low
with the snow.
Snow is as cold as ice.

Snow, snow, snow

Could be our biggest foe
all around our only found flow
all around December's glow.

Snow, snow, snow.

Parker Malone (10)
TASIS The American School In England

NOTICE

Notice . . .
The beauty of the sun,
The rhythm of the sea,
The swaying of the jungle,
The blowing of the leaves,
The falling of the stars,
They speak to me,
The playfulness of the children,
The noisiness of the city,
The echo in the valleys
The sweetness of the sugar
The prickliness of the bushes.

They speak to me
I love them too,
Because they are on my Earth.

Meredith Weber (10)
TASIS The American School In England

MY DAD

He's alright my dad,
He's as old as a tortoise,
And as nice as a rabbit,
But very bossy.
He is as wise as an owl,
He's alright my dad.
He hates chocolate,
He loves hogging the computer,
He's alright my dad.

James Wheeler (8)
The Dawnay School

WHERE DO ALL THE TEACHERS GO?

Where do all the teachers go
When it's time for bed?
Do they really have big brains
Stored inside their heads?

Do they wash up
And keep themselves clean?
Or do they just wear
Dirty old jeans?

Do they have fun
Dancing at the club?
And do they ever drink
With their friends at the pub?

So where do all the teachers go
When it's time for bed?
I really don't know,
So you think instead!

Cat Romer (10)
The Dawnay School

SNOW, SNOW

The snow is like Heaven
Drifting, drifting,
The flakes are like angels
Flying, flying,
The floor is like silk,
Shining, shining,
The trees are like sticks with
Icing, icing.

Lily Hankin (10)
The Dawnay School

THE SHADOW CAT

The shadow cat roams the street at midnight,
As she walks down the narrow passages,
Her tail like a silk, slithering snake,
Her eyes are the demons of the depths of Hell,
Knowing the every corner of the world.

The shadow cat roams the streets at midnight,
Her sharp talons go tip tap on the rough cobbled streets,
Trained for the kill.

Beware of the shadow cat,
Who roams the street at midnight,
Mysterious?
Yes, but *beware!*

Gail Commandeur (11)
The Dawnay School

MY FRIEND JOEY

My friend Joey said he could dig clear to China
I don't believe him.
My friend Joey said he was so good he got A+ million
I don't believe him.
My friend Joey said he jumped into the TV and
was on cartoons,
I don't believe him.
My friend Joey said he can turn into a sumo anytime
I don't believe him.
Joey said what he said to me was nonsense
I believe him.

Luke Rance (9)
The Dawnay School

Midnight At Nower Wood

Midnight at Nower Wood,
What do you see?
Shadows belonging to sinister beasts blocking out the moon.
Clouds in shapes of vampires' fangs slinking across the empty sky
Seeming to cackle as they go by,
'Can't catch me!'

Midnight at Nower Wood,
What do you hear?
Crackles of beastly hunters' footprints,
Fires, forgotten to be put out,
Creaks of wolves teeth ready to pounce or howl at the moon.

Midnight at Nower Wood,
What does it hide?
Thousands of people sacrificing themselves for each other
To the voice of Dracula.

Midnight at Nower Wood,
What do you feel?
You feel the door open leading to *death.*
The icy cold wind turning you to stone,
And pushing you down to the tunnel!

Amy Parr (8)
The Dawnay School

Bats At Evening

Under the husk a Scottish dusk,
Black bats scutter at high pine height,
Spluttering the night the dart and clutter,
They shake the lake bank and break as the shadows shutter,
As the damp, dark falls they cancel their calls - a large meal fuller.

Luke Culley (8)
The Dawnay School

Midnight In Nower Wood

Down in Nower Wood
In the darkness where shadows
Crept up on me
Where it creaked and the leaves
Rustled as I passed.
It was spooky,
It was haunted,
I was horrified,
Misty, spooky, evil
Shadows
Dark, damp, hollow
Trees,
They looked like monsters
From planet X.
Gloomy, misty shapes
Haunting
Shadows,
I could hear rustling,
Creaking
I could feel the chilling wind.
I couldn't hide because the
Trees surrounded me.

Robert Gray (8)
The Dawnay School

Teacher

I once had a teacher at Dawnay
Who behaved in a very strange way
She ran around like a chimp
And made a big stink
Which frightened the pupils away.

Harley Buck (10)
The Dawnay School

Midnight In Nower Wood

Darkness in the wood
Darkness in Nower Wood
What do you see?
I see the gloomy shapes creeping in the mist
I see threatening creatures swooping in the cold
Wind of the wood.
Darkness creeping through Nower Wood
What do you hear?
In the mist I hear a horrible evil haunted scary rustling sound.
Is it a monster?
Is it a ghost, or maybe a fox?

Max Denton (8)
The Dawnay School

Midnight In Nower Wood

Midnight in Nower Wood
What do you see?
Mysterious shadows creeping
Frightening *lightning* shrieking,
Figures prowling in the distant moonlight.

What do you hear?
Creaking trees rustling leaves.
Squawking owls growling.
Squeaking.
What does it hide?
Creatures creeping, crawling, scattering in the wood.

What do you feel?
Petrified, terrified, horrified
Scared it is a mysterious place.

Gareth Keen (8)
The Dawnay School

Nower Wood

Midnight in Nower Wood,
What do you see?
Dark shadows looming up in front of me,
Moonlight coming closer,
Shapeless, shapeless, haunted, haunted, horrible.

Midnight in Nower Wood,
What do you hear?
Screeching, squawking,
Howling, growling, prowling.
Hooting, hooting,
Rustling leaves, creaking trees,
Spooky.

Midnight in Nower Wood,
What does it hide?
Sinister magic,
Whispering waters,
Gushing, rushing,
The skeleton of a bat still hanging on a branch,
Creepy.

Alice Mennell (8)
The Dawnay School

How To Pass Your Cycling Proficiency

In goes gears, in goes a chain,
In goes pedals and in goes a brain.
Add a bit of oil, add a bit of rust,
Stir it all up to make it crust,
Just put this on your chest
And you will fly through the test.

Claire Cursley (11)
The Dawnay School

ZOO STRIKE

The kangaroo refused to hop,
And gave away his baby,
Now he's in the lion's hut,
Being covered in gravy.

The buffalo begins to charge,
The rhinos then join in,
So do all the antelopes,
Even though they're thin.

The leopards and tigers have swapped their coats,
It's really very confusing,
The visitors all feel as if,
Their marbles they are losing.

The zoo keepers are going mad
They really are quite barmy,
The animals are out of control,
They're calling in the army.

Nathan Farrell (10)
The Dawnay School

SNOW

Snow feels like the crunchy leaves in autumn,
Snow smells like paradise in your own back garden,
Snow looks like a neatly made bed of pure white,
Snow tastes like fresh water from a mountain spring,
When I gently tread on it it makes an echo of an eagle in
the snowy mountains.
When I am in its presence it soothes my spirit
Like the white of the snow chasing away the blackness in my life.

Sarah El-Baghdady (11)
The Dawnay School

Home Time Spell

Teachers, blackboards, boring day?
Want to be playing? No need to run away.
Here is a little home time rhyme,
Just chant this spell one thousand times.

Pencils, rubbers, want no more?
No need to lock your bedroom door,
You don't even have to write one line
Just chant this spell one thousand times.

Getting bored? Just an hour to go!
Science lesson, uh oh, oh no!
Forgot your homework? No need to hide
Just chant this spell one thousand times.

Getting close? Story time.
If you can't read don't panic it's fine.
Watching the clock, five seconds away . . . no!
Yippee! School's over! You survived the day.

Sammy Iftikhar (10)
The Dawnay School

What Is It?

First think of the person who lives in disguise,
Who deals in secrets and tells nought but lies.
Next tell me the last thing to mend, the middle of middle
And end of end.
Finally give me the sound often heard, during the search
for a hard to find word,
Now string them together and answer me this,
What animal would you be unwilling to kiss?

Fraser Aberdeen (9)
The Dawnay School

FLOWER, FLOWER

Flower, flower, shining bright,
You hold the Earth ever so tight.
As your sun-spun pollen flies away,
You cry out for water each sunny day.

Flower, flower, calm and tight,
You face the sun keen and bright.
You face the rain, wind and hail,
Sometimes you turn ever so pale.

Flower, flower, how you nod,
You were once a tiny, tiny bud.
Your petals are red, violet and blue,
And you're scent is like the morning dew.

Flower, flower, it has come to your end,
Slowly you wither and slowly you bend.
First your petals drop to the ground,
None of them make a single sound.

Anusha Young (9)
The Dawnay School

SNOW DAY

Snowflakes fall into children's mouths,
Tingling their tastebuds,
I can hear icicles smash onto the ground,
We pull out of the drive slowly, steadily.
Being careful not to slip or slide.
Snowflakes pour onto houses like cream,
Poured onto chocolate cake.
Families snuggle round warm fires thinking
About the cold.

Kerrina Gray (10)
The Dawnay School

My Best Pussy In The Whole Wide World

Let me tell you about my cat
Just pretend
She is also your friend
Let's sit and have a chat.

She prowls by night and loves her food
Her name is Maddie she is a cool dude
She's my little friend and on my bed
She rests her soft and furry head.

She's out at night chasing little mice
She's very good, she's caught one twice
I do love my cat in every way
In my sweet care I hope she'll stay.

Rebecca Jones (8)
The Dawnay School

All Through The Day

The sun shines in the early morning sky,
Like a golden ball floating
And smells like a bunch of fresh flowers,
The clouds move delicately
Bouncing in the sunlit mist,
The day moves on, dawn to dusk,
The moon comes into the foggy sky,
The walls are as cold as ice,
A wind gently blows all around,
The day is over, goodnight.

Amanda Apps (10)
The Dawnay School

MY FRIEND ROSS

My friend Ross said he jumped off a cliff
And he did not die.
I don't believe him.

My friend Ross said he swam two miles
And he was the champion.
I don't believe him.

My friend Ross said he could dive off the top diving board
And not break his back.
I don't believe him.

My friend Ross said his grandad got killed by a glass
Of lemonade and poison.
I don't believe him.

My friend Ross said he tried to jump a mile
And got halfway there.
I don't believe him.

My friend Ross said he could do one hundred press-ups
In forty night seconds and he did not fail.
I do believe him.

Daniel Leach (10)
The Dawnay School

SNAKES

Sly, sloshing, slithering snakes
Snakes slither in a river,
Sly, slosh, slither snake
Sly snakes slosh, slither in a river
Not a single snake must dither.

Julia Smith (9)
The Dawnay School

My Friend

My friend Matilda says that she can jump up to space.
I don't believe her.

My friend Matilda says that she can fly like a bird.
I don't like her.

My friend Matilda says that she can stay underwater
for two hours.
I don't believe her.

My friend Matilda says that she can ski on her hands.
I don't believe her.

My friend Matilda says that she could read a book at five years old.
I believe her.

Jessica Leitch (10)
The Dawnay School

My Cat

He crouches,
Eyes gleaming,
Ready to pounce.
He moves slowly, but softly.
He eyes his prize.
It's time.
He jumps and lands,
Bang!
I've always wondered why my cat
likes attacking bubbles!

Sophie Clowser (10)
The Dawnay School

SNOWDAY

On snowday when I get up
And the clock goes *dong*
I go and stare outside
And sing the little song.

Snow, snow wonderful snow
Pale against the sky
Snow snow wonderful snow
I see the clouds cry.

Snow, snow beautiful snow
The Earth is like a snow dome
Snow, snow beautiful snow
It feels as soft as foam.

Snow, snow brilliant snow
Houses topped with icing
Snow, snow brilliant snow
Through the air it's slicing.

Snow, snow excellent snow
Falling in tiny flakes
Snow, snow excellent snow
The theme of a thousand Christmas cakes.

Snow, snow glorious snow
From a flour shaker
Snow, snow glorious snow
I bless the maker.

Jack Denton (10)
The Dawnay School

FRIEND

My friend Bill says he can fit 981178
Chocolates in his mouth at once and not get sick.
I don't believe him.

My friend Bill says he can run faster than a cheetah
Without getting attacked or getting tired.
I don't believe him.

My friend Bill says he can pick up two whole buildings
Without hurting his back.
I don't believe him.

My friend Bill says he can write 91178 pages
Without stopping and his hand aching.
I don't believe him.

My friend says he can swim fifty lengths without stopping.
I believe him.

Anthony Bligh (10)
The Dawnay School

SNOW

As soft as cotton wool,
As keen as a frostbite,
As light as the disappearing air,
Pirouettes like a ballerina.

As white as the springing blossom,
As delicate as the newborn baby,
As exciting as opening your Christmas or
Birthday presents,
Tiny snowflakes falling, falling.

Cherry Cattermole (10)
The Dawnay School

SLEEP LITTLE FLOWER, SLEEP

Sleep little flower, sleep
When the bright morning
Comes you will shine like
The sky.

Sleep little flower, sleep
When I wake you up you
Will be happy and your
Colour will show.

Sleep little flower, sleep
When I go out in the garden
I will smile at you
And play.

Sleep little flower, sleep
When the night falls you will
Close your eyes and
Dream of the morning.

Sleep little flower, sleep
When I go to school I
Will remember you and
Comfort you when I get
Home.

Sleep little flower, sleep
When it's summer and
There's no rain I will come
Out and water you and you'll
Shine like the stars in the
Midnight sky.

Laura Cronin (9)
The Dawnay School

The Policeman

In a decreased dark suit a policeman stands,
Trying to stop people dropping their cans.
Hand in his pocket, cap under arm,
He stands there stock still preventing crime.
He's strutting around checking car tickets,
And stopping some people doing some knick-its.
He's a safety policeman looking and looking,
For people who want him to check their bookings.
The policeman helps those in need,
And stops people with great greed.

Emma Houslander (9)
The Dawnay School

Daydreaming

I daydream in the window thinking, *I am the champ.*
I daydream I can change anything anywhere.
I see you and me everywhere in a bloom of blossoms
Tied up in a bouquet of joy.
I see you in the sunshine smiling the whole day, away
Flowed by a cheerful grin.
In a child's smile I see that joyful face.
In a stormful sky I can still see the hope that you alone can bring.
In the classroom I can see the happiness flying out of the
open door as everyone rushes out for break.

Mariam El-Baghdady (8)
The Dawnay School

Riding My Bike

Riding my bike, on a hike,
What do you think I see?
A cat sitting on a doorstep,
Someone I've never met.

Riding my bike, on a hike,
What do you think I see?
A child playing in the park,
Someone dressed very smart.

Riding my bike, on a hike,
What do you think I see?
I see a rippling pond,
And in that pond
I see *me!*

Rebecca Lambert (9)
The Dawnay School

The Snake

The hideous snake slides across the room.
The snake's eyes shine in the moonlight,
His black skin is smooth and scaly,
He slides across the floor.

This reptile slowly opens his mouth
And shows his vampire fangs.
His tongue is as red as blood,
The creature bites his prey.

Alex Rollins (9)
The Dawnay School

Billy Brand

There was a little boy,
His name was Billy Brand,
He said, 'No matter how I try,
I can't walk on my hands!
I flick my legs into the air,
Point them straight and high,
It never ever works though,
They don't stay in the sky!
I collapse in a heap in the floor,
I'll try another day,
Maybe I'll just use a wall,
Or walk the proper way.'

Catherine Ryder (10)
The Dawnay School

What Am I?

I am in a lullaby,
I reach up to the sky,
My hair is thick and green
But in autumn has an auburn sheen.
My little cups are overfilled,
My hair falls out when I am chilled.
My skin is wrinkly and tough,
My arms are long and rough.
Squirrels often bury my fruits,
And if forgotten they come up as shoots,
My shoots are there but slowly growing,
How old they will get there is just no knowing,
What am I?

Chloe Walker-Trivett (9)
The Dawnay School

The Sound Collector

(Based on 'The Sound Collector' by Roger McGough)

A stranger called this morning,
Dressed all in black and grey,
Put every sound into a bag,
And carried them away.

The whistling of the wind,
The turning of the TV volume,
The purring of the motorbike starting,
The ticking of my teacher marking my homework.

The popping of a Wonka bar in my mouth,
The crunching of my toast being eaten,
The scraping of my dad doing woodwork,
The hissing of the baby's rattle.

The bubbling of my fish in their tank,
The drumming of my heart as I watch my favourite horror movie,
The gurgle of my sister as she washes her mouth,
The crying of injured animals.

The squeaking of the stairs as I jump down them,
The swishing of the leaves on a windy day,
The creaking of the loft as my mum climbs up.

A stranger called this morning,
He didn't leave his name,
Left us only silence,
Life will never be the same.

Natalie Goodacre (9)
The Dawnay School

My Friend Jake

My friend Jake G said his dad is the President
And he gets £10,000 from him every day
I don't believe him.

My friend Jake G said he has a secret lab in his
Back garden hidden in his shed and has discovered
A cure for cancer.
I don't believe him.

My friend Jake G said he can fly high in the sky and
Can talk to animals.
I don't believe him.

My friend Jake G said he plays for Chelsea
And won the Premier League.
I don't believe him.

My friend Jake G said he has super powers and
He had saved the world from comets.
I don't believe him.

My friend Jake G said he can do 74 kick-ups and plays
For the Under 10s for Fulham.
I believe him.

Toby Irwin (10)
The Dawnay School

Riddle

I silence all cries,
I take away pain,
I destroy suffering,
Yet I cause grief.
What am I?

Daniel Morrison (10)
The Dawnay School

Red Caterpillar And White Caterpillar

Red and white on a wet winter night,
Driving home from work
You can see red caterpillar and white caterpillar,
Slithering down silver, slippery trails.
Heading in different directions.

Red and white on a wet winter night,
When the rain is pounding, thrashing at your windscreen,
You can see red caterpillar and white caterpillar,
Dragging their bodies of luminous lights
Through the dark and stormy night.

Red and white on a wet winter night,
When menacing bridges and spooky trees surround a well-
trodden path,
You can see red caterpillar and white caterpillar,
Sliding beneath a pitch black bucket
That leaks.

Red and white on a wet winter night,
When it's getting very late.
You can see red caterpillar and white caterpillar,
Parts of which are turning off at junctions and rolling into
Their drives to have a well-earned rest.

David Andrews (9)
The Dawnay School

My Dad

My dad is all right
He tickles me 'til I can laugh no more
My dad is special to me
My dad loves me.

Ben Fisher (8)
The Dawnay School

I Don't Believe Him

My friend Ben says he can read my thoughts,
His brother has glasses that make him invisible,
He can jump in front of lorries and not die or get hurt.
I don't believe him.

My friend Ben says he can fly
And he has laser beam eyes.
I don't believe him.

My friend Ben says he is in the FBI and
He is an undercover agent with loads of cool weapons and stuff.
I don't believe him.

My friend Ben says he is cool,
Good at football and supports Chelsea
I do believe him.

Ed Anstis (10)
The Dawnay School

My Friend Helen

My friend Helen says she can sneeze
Fifty times in a second.
I don't believe her.

My friend Helen says she can fly over
Five elephants in one swish of a wing.
I don't believe her.

My friend Helen says she can jump
Up to Pluto and back.
I don't believe her.

My friend Helen says she was not telling the truth.
I believe her.

Anita Massimo (9)
The Dawnay School

My Friend Josh

My friend Josh says he is a football player
And can beat David Beckham with his hands behind
His back
I don't believe him.

My friend Josh says he can beat The Rock with
His little toe and win
I don't believe him.

My friend Josh says he is the strongest man alive
And can lift up the world in his hands.
I don't believe him.

My friend Josh says he can drop in off a pipe
And mickflip into Indie.
I don't believe him.

My friend Josh says he goes skateboarding and can dive
I believe him.

Robert Cunnett (10)
The Dawnay School

My Sister

When my sister's sleeping,
You can't wake her without her weeping.
She'll get out of bed shouting
And if you're not careful, she'll start clouting.
If she's in a bad mood she'll start spitting
Even while she's doing her knitting.
While playing a game she's mean,
But while doing her homework, she's a killing machine.

Ella Smith (9)
The Dawnay School

WHERE DO ALL THE TEACHERS GO?

Do they belong to the FBI
or do they belong to an evil mob?
Are they undercover cops
and do they try to rob?

Are they aliens?
Do they come from Mars?
Do they have a different form
And do they like red cars?

Have they got real names
And do they know how to fly?
Can they read well
And do they ever lie?

James Woodley (10)
The Dawnay School

WHERE DO ALL THE TEACHERS GO?

Do all the teachers meet up and go to the shops
Or do they go straight home into bed?
Do they get drunk and get caught by the cops
Do they have a mate called Ned?

Do they go to discos
Or sit on the sofa and eat?
Do they even go to Tesco's
And do they have extremely smelly feet?

Do they like Fanta
Or are they marking school work?
Do they have a pet Manta?
They are 100% berserk.

Ross Elliott (9)
The Dawnay School

Teachers

Do teachers go clubbing
or do they stick to the gym?
Or do they end up sitting in
an old tin bin?

Do they go to the parlour
to buy some fake tan?
Or do they do on the Internet
to get a cute man?

Do teachers use their heads
or do they use a calculator?
I think they just go to bed
and pray for later.

Where do all the teachers go
after ten-fifteen?
Are they making themselves clear?
I really haven't seen!

Juliet Grenville (9)
The Dawnay School

My Dad

My dad is cuddly
My dad is nice
My dad tickles me a lot
My dad likes cooking
My dad likes playing on his computer
My dad likes doing sport
My dad likes watching football
My dad plays with me.

Charlotte Black (8)
The Dawnay School

My Best Friend

Would your best friend call you up at night?
Would he help you in a fight?
Would he give you his last sweet?
Would he let you on his bike?
Mine did.

Would your best friend hit you in a fight?
Would your best friend leave you alone?
Would your best friend say bad things behind your back?
Mine didn't.

Would your best friend help you in a maths problem?
Would your bet friend be there for you?
Would a best friend let you sleep over at his house?
Mine did.

Would your best friend be nasty?
Would your best friend hurt you?
Mine doesn't.
My friend for ever.

Josh Rapley (9)
The Dawnay School

My Dad

He's brilliant is my dad.
He usually gives me treats,
He is slow as a snail,
He is as strict as a teacher,
He is as fun as a computer,
He is as soft and cuddly as a feather,
He is as good as a DIY builder.

Madeleine Halls (8)
The Dawnay School

My Best Friend

My friend Jake G said he could invent
Superpower bouncy buildings and make it shrink so
small that you cannot see it.
I don't believe him.

My friend Jake G said he could fly around the world in
a millisecond and land back in the same spot.
I don't believe him.

My friend Jake G said he had a trip to Uranus and then
he went back to the sun to get tanned.
I don't believe him.

My friend Jake G said he could disappear and say it was
a magic trick when it wasn't
I don't believe him.

My friend Jake G said he plays for Fulham and can do skills
and tricks and make people laugh.
I believe him.

Harriet Connor (10)
The Dawnay School

What Am I?

I am rather gorgeous and colourful
With a smell that's pretty wonderful.
Bees won't leave me alone
Especially when I'm fully grown.
I am very clever,
I can make my own food forever.
To keep me happy and beautiful and smelling sweetly too,
Give me lots of water and I'll make you happy too!

Stephanie Law (9)
The Dawnay School

My Friend

My friend Summer says she fell off a thirty storey
houseblock and survived.
I don't believe her.

My friend Summer said she said supercalafragalisticexpalidotios
when she was only one day old.
I don't believe her.

My friend Summer said she put a ruler up her nose for
two hours and pulled it out again with her tongue.
I don't believe her.

My friend Summer says she had a trip to Mars and had Coke
with the aliens.
I don't believe her.

My friend Summer said her mum's had a baby brother.
I do believe her.

Elizabeth Childes (9)
The Dawnay School

A Snake

I saw a snake slithering over a log,
I saw a snake swirling and twirling through trees.
I saw a snake catch a prey cautiously,
I saw a snake hiss and hiss angrily,
I saw a snake camouflage quickly under some leaves,
I saw a snake zoom past my steady feet,
I saw a snake swerve round a sharp corner,
I saw a snake slowly and silently drift off to Heaven.

William Learmont (8)
The Dawnay School

My Best Friends

Do your best friends . . .
Help you when you fall over,
Pass to you in football,
Let you join in their games,
And cheer you up when you are sad?
Mine do!

Do your best friends . . .
Share their toys with you,
Invite you round to their house,
Let you play their computer games,
And hang out with you?
Mine do!

Do your best friends . . .
Push you about and make you sad,
Leave you out of all their games
Call you horrible names,
And say they don't like you?
Mine don't!

Ben Bedford (10)
The Dawnay School

The Tiger Cinquain

Sneaking
Creeping tiger
As quiet as a mouse
I'm waiting to pounce on my prey
Fear me.

Maria Tilt (10)
The Dawnay School

My Friend Juliet

My friend Juliet says she can win the London Marathon
by miles and still not be tired.
I don't believe her.

My friend Juliet says she could beat the world record any day
but she's not allowed to run.
I don't believe her.

My friend Juliet says she can sing better than Tatu
I don't believe her.

My friend Juliet says she's the President's daughter.
I don't believe her.

My friend Juliet says she's kind, funny and she is a good friend.
I believe her.

Jenny Pemberton (10)
The Dawnay School

Snake

A slithering snake
Wriggling-a-wiggling
Through the grass.
He sheds his colourful
patterned skin.
His fangs spitting
a purple poisonous spit.
While he wriggles-a-wriggles
through the grass.

Iona Doig (8)
The Dawnay School

My Friend

My friend Belinda says she made a walking loo,
If you need the loo it will come to you.
I don't believe her.

My friend Belinda says that she jumps over ten cars
In two seconds.
I don't believe her.

My friend Belinda says that she can sit for one whole day
And not get tired or hungry.
I don't believe her.

My friend Belinda says that sometimes she tells lies.
I believe her.

Rachel Cumper (9)
The Dawnay School

My Dad

My dad can jump as high as a bunny
My dad can lift me up with one hand
My dad is as fit as a pin
My dad hates getting stuck in traffic jams
My dad loves drinking beer
My dad is excellent at football, he can do three million kick ups.
My dad can make me laugh and scream till I cry
My dad gives me loads of sweets when we go on a long car journey.
My dad can run like the wind
My dad is exactly like a super hero
I love my dad and guess what, he loves me!

Rianne Elliott (8)
The Dawnay School

WHERE DO ALL THE TEACHERS GO?

Where do all the teachers go
at the end of school?
Do they wear pjs
that say Elvis Presley rules?

Where do all the teachers go
when the day does end?
Do they have a teddy bear?
They must have gone round the bend.

So I followed one home one night
and this is what I saw.
A teacher with a teddy bear
and they were thirty-four!

Are they really teachers
or do they just pretend?
At that age it wasn't good at all
but do they have a friend?

Where do all the teachers go
at the end of school?
I thought that all they thought about
were rules, rules, rules!

Rebecca Dawson (9)
The Dawnay School

DINOSAUR'S TEETH

On a hot, hot day a dinosaur will say,
'Roar' when its tooth gets sore.
Now we've invented toothpaste which humans
will hate,
And dinos will love forever more.

George Chard (8)
The Dawnay School

THE SNOW

We were in the classroom
about to go out to play.
I could not wait
the trees were twizzling
shooting the snow
so you could see the bare, brown,
brass branches.
I walked over the snow
crunch, crunch,
I felt like I was walking
on a clean duvet off my bed.
I threw a cold snowball,
and my hat, gloves and coat got soaked.
I had never seen snow like this before.

Joanna Russell (8)
The Dawnay School

MIDNIGHT AT NOWER WOOD

I could see in the gloomy night
There were shadows on the moonlight.

There were trees which looked like they had faces.

I had never been to such scary places.
The branches looked like they had hands with spikes.
I felt I could ride away on my bike.

I could hear an owl hooting and a wolf howling.
I looked around and heard something gentle growling.
I could see a haunted house on the hill.
I kept very still.

Samuel Hudson (8)
The Dawnay School

MIDNIGHT IN NOWER WOOD

I can see the rustling branches,
I can see the shooting stars above.
What's that noise?
There, coming towards me was a deer!
He saw me watching him
he looked at me with his big black eyes
sparkling with light.
An owl hooted far away.

Alexandra Sarah Hastie (8)
The Dawnay School

ONE-EYED JAKE

In dark of night with full moon shining,
Jake and his crew sat there dining,
On their ship sailing on,
With Captain Jake's beard so long.

So cheerful were the crew of Jake's
All with one eye and a tattoo of a snake,
As all had beer and food and wealth,
But Jake was worried about his health.

One day Jake knew he would wither and die,
He then scrunched in a corner and began to cry,
Jake was weak and old,
And lay there cold.

Lewis Andrews (10)
The Dawnay School

WINTER'S MORNING

Snow
As cold as a helpless mouse on
a winter's morning
as white as a winter holiday.

Snow
It saunters down the deep blue sky
then lays on the floor
like paint being splattered in slow motion.

Snow
Like something I have never seen before
as bright as the sun that never shines.

Snow
I hope it never leaves
because of the wonderful thing it is.

Thomas Dicks (10)
The Dawnay School

MORE SCHOOL FOR WITCH

Crickle, crackle, spit and *splat*
Lots more school for me to have
Into the kiln a box of rulers
Many lunchtimes and roasted dinners
Add in coach trips and some rubbers
Pots of pencils and evil teachers,
Heat the kiln up until it burns.

Wish come true, more half terms for me.

Charlotte Bateman (11)
The Dawnay School

THE MOUSE WHO LIVES IN MY HOUSE

I've seen a mouse in my house.
He comes to play every day
He eats some cheese and has a pee
He runs away across the mat.
To get away from the hungry cat.

The cat licks his paws
And runs out of the door
To chase the mouse
Who's left the house.

I look to the sky
An owl catches my eye
He's seen the mouse
Who ran out of the house
He flaps his wings
And dives and sings.
Tu-whit, tu-whoo, tu-whit, tu-whoo
The moon is bright
The mouse runs out of sight.
The owl flies away
And the mouse lives for another day!

Jade Leach (11)
The Dawnay School

SNOW

Snowflakes fall like feathers caught by the wind,
Bare trees standing tall with fluffy soft cream,
The roofs covered perfectly in smooth icing,
My toes like blocks of ice, crunching over the snow,
Excitement filling the morning with joy,
Snow, if only it would stay forever.

Elizabeth Pymm (11)
The Dawnay School

THE WISH FAIRY

Wish fairy! Wish fairy! with your long golden wings!
Grant me a wish
Oh! wish fairy!

Wish fairy! Wish fairy! with your soft, white hair!
Grant me a wish,
Oh! wish fairy!

Wish fairy! Wish fairy! your eyes are like diamonds,
Grant me a wish,
Oh! wish fairy!

Wish fairy! Wish fairy! your voice is so sweet
Grant me a wish,
Oh! wish fairy!

Wish fairy! Wish fairy! I love your name Lavender
Grant me a wish,
Oh! wish fairy!

A silken dress, the colour bright pink and crystals made into a heart
That's what I wish for!
Oh! wish fairy!

Lucy Hunt (8)
The Dawnay School

CHAMELEON CINQUAIN

I'm a
Chameleon,
Bright red, slurping, long tongue,
Changing colour chameleon,
Spots, stripes.

Katherine Hughes (9)
The Dawnay School

Roller Coaster

Let's go to the roller coaster
With its winding tracks
We will see if we'll survive in time for tea and snacks.
Jump into the cart and get the best two seats
We want to be first to see the amazing feats.
Well here it comes the bars are coming down
Now I have got that nasty feeling deep, deep inside.
Up, up, up we go I can really feel that wind blow.
Now we are zooming in the sky,
Letting fear fly by.
Phew, it's just about to stop
Now I think I'm going to pop!

Rose Williams (8)
The Dawnay School

River Poem

At a river there's water
speeding down a high
cliff like rain raging to the ground.

At a river there are animals
rushing to drink the ice-cold water
like a shepherd in a race.

At a river there's shiny rocks
glowing out of the water
like the reflection of the moon.

Michael Black (9)
The Dawnay School

MY NAN

My nan is so groovy
She likes watching movies
Her dance is so funny
She likes wasting money.
She's a marvellous cook
Her head's always in a book.
She's a very nice cuddler,
And she's always in a muddler.
She's such a groovy chick,
She does not take the mick.
She's a very sweet Nan you ought to know
    And that's why I love my very nice Nan so.

Emma Paige (9)
The Dawnay School

STRANGE THINGS

Old man's eyes, child's face,
Watching as the shadows race,
In and out the cracks,
Running in the winter's sun,
So the night will leave today.

Old town, dirty street,
Walked around by shoeless feet,
Tall concrete buildings,
Nearly every side you'll see,
Those concrete monsters they'll be.

Cameron Fox (10)
The Dawnay School

WHAT AM I?

What kind of goose
Has a long tail?
What kind of goose
Eats eggs?
What kind of goose
Is brown?
What kind of goose
Lives in water?
Can you guess what I am?
(Mongoose)

Rebecca Coles (10)
The Dawnay School

TIGERS CINQUAIN

I am
dressed in stripes
I can and will hunt you
for in the tree tops I can see
the ground.

Beth Woodham (10)
The Dawnay School

JESS

There once was a girl called Jess,
Who's mouth was a terrible mess,
She once opened it wide,
Out came a tide,
And seagulls had nested in her vest.

Kristian Eaton (9)
The Dawnay School

APOSTROPHE POEM

Best remembered:
My sister's smile,
My friend's helpfulness,
My aunt's joke,
My dad's laughter,
My mum's helpfulness.

Best forgotten:
My goldfish's death
My sister's moodiness,
My other sister's crawling,
My friend's crossness with me,
My guinea pig's bite
My mum's madness.

Janet Foskett (9)
Woodside Junior School

APOSTROPHE POEM

Best remembered:
My dog's sloppiness
My cat's purriness
My nan's tears
My grandad's stinky feet!
My mum's snacks

Best forgotten:
My sister's long nails
My mum's best outfit
My grandad's snoring
My brother's broken nose
My friend's bad day.

Charlie Penfold (8)
Woodside Junior School

APOSTROPHE POEM

Best remembered:
My cat's big eyes.
My dog's fluffy ears.
My mum's happiness.
My brother's tallness.
My dad's cheerfulness.
My gran's spag bol
My friend's laughter.

Best forgotten:
My cat's sharp claws.
My gran's boring house.
My mum's casserole.
My best friend's lying.
My brother's fights.
My dad's big spot.
My brother's horridness.

Ross Marshall (8)
Woodside Junior School

THINGS TO REMEMBER AND FORGET

My dog's first walk
My dog who barks at thin air
My dog's fierce growls
My first snowman
Leaving my old friends
My argument with my best friends
My dog's sharp teeth.

Ellie Burtenshaw (9)
Woodside Junior School

The Plane Delay

I was looking through my window,
One fine and sunny day,
When I remembered watching the news last week,
And I found out about a plane delay.

I pictured all those angry people
Shouting and punching the air,
And I thought about how I would feel,
If I saw them there.

I thought about how I would feel,
If I was one of them,
And how I would feel,
If I was one of them hardworking men.

If I was the one being punched,
I'd probably feel angry,
And how much it would hurt,
All the rest of my family.

I continued looking out of my window,
Thinking about the plane delay,
And how I'd feel if it was happening to me,
On this fine and sunny day.

Sian Fitzpatrick (9)
Woodside Junior School

Rubber Haiku

Roughly rubbing out
In the pot waiting again
Roughly rubbing out.

Thomas Bean (10)
Woodside Junior School

Apostrophe Poem

Best remembered:
My cat's small eyes,
My dog's floppy ears,
My mum's warm touch,
My dad's funny jokes,
My sister's first smile,
My other sister's laugh,
My best friend's attitude.

Best forgotten:
My cat's upturned face,
My dog's sloppy tongue,
My mum's big smacks,
My dad's cross voice,
My sister's crying,
My other sister's whinging,
My best friend's arguing.

Priyel Upadhyaya (8)
Woodside Junior School

Merchant Ship

Gliding across the water,
Selling pots, bags and a mortar,
Sailing into the port of Dover,
Just as the sails turn over.

Gliding across the water,
Selling rugs, weapons and a mortar,
Sailing into the port of Kong
Just as the clock goes *bong!*

Tom Barry (10)
Woodside Junior School

APOSTROPHE POEM

Best remembered:
My mum's cuddle
My aunty's laughter,
My dad's Guinness,
My friend's jokes,
My cat's loving fur,
My gran's stories,
My uncle's talent.

Best forgotten:
My mum's shouting,
My gran's cooking,
My cat's miaowing,
My dad's snoring,
My friend's silliness,
My uncle's beard.

Geoffrey Whitby (8)
Woodside Junior School

TEDDY BEAR'S QUESTIONS

Hello teddy how are you?
And how do you do?
Have you been to the park?
Did you get a good mark?
How was school?
Did you have a good game of ball?
How are your friends?
Did you buy some pens?
Oh teddy bear are you tired?
Are you sleepy?
Well it's time for beddy teddy!

Teri Bailey (10)
Woodside Junior School

Apostrophe Poem

Best remembered:
My sister's soft skin,
My mum's warm touch,
My dad's funny laugh,
My grandma's nice cooking,
My brother's trainers,
My best friend's kindness.

Best forgotten:
My sister's sharp nails,
My mum's bad outfits,
My dad's big spot,
My grandma's tiny telly,
My brother's nosiness,
My best friend's messy room.

Naomi Harrison (9)
Woodside Junior School

What I Think!

I think alot about girlie girls,
While I play with curly whirls.
Act like Rianna
While I watch Dianna.
Roses in a bush
While I sing wushy wush.
There are swimmers
And they're winners.
What a sight
In the night.
And that's what I think.

Mariam Farooqui (10)
Woodside Junior School

APOSTROPHE

Best remembered:
My mum's happy times,
My dad's worst days,
My fish's clever eating,
My dog's lovely hair,
My best friend's smile,
My brother's laughter,
My mum's loveliness.

Best forgotten:
My dog's scratching noise,
My brother's smelly feet,
My mum's long fingernails,
My dad's shouting,
My sister's crying,
My friend's being smelly,
My sister's calling.

Christopher Newlyn (9)
Woodside Junior School

THE OLYMPIC GAMES

A swimmer is a dolphin
A sprinter is a spring
A weightlifter is a gorilla
A pole-vaulter is a swing
A wrestler is a bear,
A long jumper is a frog,
A gymnast is a monkey,
A rower is a log.

Cristie Jarvis (10)
Woodside Junior School

APOSTROPHE POEM

Best remembered:
My cat's soft and thick fur,
My mum's short hair,
My dad's fingers when he tickles me,
My sister's small, messy room,
My grandad's plant and bird books,
My nan's video collection,
My aunty's wallpaper,
My uncle's computer service.

Best forgotten:
My cat's cough,
My mum's washing when she forgets to turn it on.
My dad's moaning,
My sister's cheesy smile,
My grandad's glasses,
My nan's book collection,
My aunty's house,
My uncle's garden.

Georgina Amor (8)
Woodside Junior School

THE MOON

The moon is like a banana all mashed up and made into stew.
It's like a smile that is always there.
It never goes unless it's full.
It's like a melon on a plate.
It's like a carrot that's been peeled.
It's half a mango on a plate.
It never leaves the sky.

Leanne Walker (9)
Woodside Junior School

Apostrophe Poem

Best remembered:
My cat's soft fluffy tail,
My rabbit's fluffy head,
My brother's funny beard,
My dad's cuddly arms,
My grandad's snooker table,
My hamster getting out of his cage so I can hold him,
My best friend's joke.

Best forgotten:
My cat's bite,
My rabbit getting lost,
My brother's messy room,
My dad's yelling,
My grandad's bad outfit,
My hamster gnawing at his cage,
My best friend's cross face.

Harry Wall (9)
Woodside Junior School

Haunted School Room

I was teaching in an old school room
And a werewolf drove in on a motorbike
With a broom
I saw a headless mouse
Then a vampire came in with a house
I said, 'Go away!' And it ran to its tomb.

Ashley Sullivan (10)
Woodside Junior School

Apostrophe Poem

Best remembered:
My brother's special toy,
My dad's blue car,
My mum's old red cooker,
My little brother's toy car,
My uncle's motorbike,
My grandad's old TV,
My granma's old bed,
My best friend's skill.

Best forgotten:
My dog's evil eyes,
My brother's dirty bike,
My dad's stinky socks,
My mum's old bruise,
My little brother's long coat,
My uncle's big spot,
My best friend's fighting.

Asif Ali (8)
Woodside Junior School

Dark Long Shed

I was in the dark, long shed
When a man rode in, without a head
I said, 'Shoo!'
So he hid in the loo
And I went back to the shed.

Ross Goodey (10)
Woodside Junior School

APOSTROPHE POEM

Best remembered:
My cat's rats,
My fish's calmness
My dad's football match
My mum's washing
My brother's bed,
My nan's apple pie
And my grandad's soft fingers.

Best forgotten:
My cat's sharp claws,
My fish's bubble noises,
My dad's rock voice,
My mum's dusting,
My brother's kick boxing,
My nan's favourite dress,
And my grandad's friends.

Samantha Porter (8)
Woodside Junior School

CHRISTMAS

C hristmas is very near
H oping I've got what I want
R eindeer are cute
I like Father Christmas
S anta is near
T rees are picking now
M um says, 'Go to sleep.' But I say 'No.'
A re you like me?
S now is falling like flour.

Hannah Rossi (9)
Woodside Junior School

Apostrophe Poem

Best remembered:
My mum's beautiful smile,
My hamster's soft squeak,
My brother's loud laugh,
My dad's terrible singing,
My gran's beautiful cooking,
My grandpa's corny jokes,
My dog's cold nose.

Best forgotten:
My mum's terrible sadness,
My hamster's death,
My brother's cry,
My dad's thunderous snoring,
My gran's terrible shout,
My grandpa's cold feet,
My dog's hot nose.

Holly Sud (9)
Woodside Junior School

The Moon

The moon is a piece
of Terry's Chocolate Orange.

The moon is a side of someone
staring at something.

The moon is a ready
to eat banana.

The moon is a curved
finger pointing at something.

Ben Lawson (10)
Woodside Junior School

Apostrophe Poem

Best remembered:
My cat's funny *purrrr*,
My sister's silly talk,
My teacher's games,
My mum's lovely voice,
My dad's fun and games,
My dog's wet nose,
My best friend's giggle.

Best forgotten:
My cat's rotten times
My sister's boring games
My gran's tiny house
My mum's sloppy kiss
My dad's too much caring
My dog's loud bark
My best friend's arguments.

Alexandra Kelland (9)
Woodside Junior School

The Crescent Moon

The moon is a spoiler shining in a little light
The moon is Terry's Chocolate Orange, all creamy inside
The moon is a twisting snake, all slimy and scaly
The moon is a banana, always yellow
The moon is a golden bracelet that will never end
The moon is a golden helmet ready for a hero
The moon is a tail of a big Sheffield dog
The moon is a letter C for candy
The moon is a skipping rope going round and round
The moon is moon forever.

Nikisha Cantle (10)
Woodside Junior School

Water

Water goes *pop* in Portugal
Water goes *whoosh* in Wales,
Water goes *splosh* in Spain.
Water goes *drip* in Denmark
Water goes *pitter-patter* in Peru
Water goes *splish* in Sweden
Water goes *ripple* in Russia
Water goes *gush* in Germany
Water flows in France
Water evaporates in Equador
Water condenses in Canada
Water boils in Bolivia
Water freezes in Finland
Water showers in Slovakia
Water runs in Romania
Water pours in Poland.

James Giddy (9)
Woodside Junior School

The Crescent Moon

The moon is a mouth from somebody's face.
The moon is a piece of orange chocolate.
The moon is a big banana from someone's fruit bowl.
The moon is like a big boomerang.
The moon is a spoiler from a car.
The moon is like an overgrown toenail.
The moon is like a bendy ruler.
The moon is just a plain old moon.

George Davis (9)
Woodside Junior School

THE CRESCENT MOON

The crescent moon is like . . .
A big slice of Terry's Snowball Chocolate Orange
A ripe yellow banana
And a sideways smile.

The crescent moon is like . . .
A lemon in a big bowl
A orange cut into sixths
And like a toenail floating in a drink.

The crescent moon is like . . .
A basketball cut into lots of pieces
A slice of cheese
And like a star in the universe.

Kalifa Best (9)
Woodside Junior School

THE LION

The lion woke up
And took his cup
Went downstairs
Fed the bears
Went outside
To play on his slide
Went back in
Fell in the bin
Got in the bath
And washed the calf
He went to bed
And bumped his head
Oh that silly old lion.

Emily Mills (9)
Woodside Junior School

WET PLAY TIME

Wet play time is so much fun,
Drawing pictures with everyone.
Splitter, splatter,
Splitter, splatter.
Playing games like draughts or chess,
Reading books or watching cress.
Brenda's dirtied her new dress!
Drip, drop,
Drip, drop,
Screams and shouts and pushing over,
Looking on a map for Dover.
Billy's found a four-leaved clover.
Pitter-patter,
Pitter-patter.
Looking at books about England's plumbing,
You can hear the school band drumming.
Everyone - quick the teacher's coming!
Trickle . . . ickle . . .
Trickle . . . ickle . . .
'Hello class you can go out to play.
The rain has stopped.'
Everyone shouts . . .
'*Yeahhhhh!*'

David Parke (9)
Woodside Junior School

The Crescent Moon

The moon is a banana
about to be eaten
rotten and smelly
and hairy and green.

The moon is a football
being kicked around and around
it has just been kicked in the goal
and kicked back out again.

The moon is a birthday cake
ready to dig into
it has green icing on top
and it tastes like chocolate.

The moon is a knife
sharp and pointy
its blade is shiny
enough to kill.

The moon is a boomerang
hard as wood
it has sharp and pointed edges
and you can throw it very high.

James Hatfield (9)
Woodside Junior School

The Crescent Moon

The moon is a banana
floating in the air
all squishy and gooey
and a mouldy piece of fruit.

The moon is a slice of lemon
floating in a cool drink
with a very sweet taste
and is a very bright fruit.

The moon is a boomerang
as bent as a twig
as fast as a leopard
and as colourful as a clown.

The moon is a sword
as sharp as a blade
cutting through the jungle
as shiny as a gold ring.

The moon is a flat football
as floppy as a pillow
black and white like Newcastle
and as rubbery as leather.

Aaron Keefe (9)
Woodside Junior School

WHAT I WOULD WANT IN MY SOUND BOX

(Based on 'Magic Box' by Kit Wright)

In my sound box I would put . . .
The sound of burning fire crackling in the fireplace
The sound of the howling and whistling of the air
passing down my street
The sound of my baby cousin crying whenever he's being fed
The sound of my mum's jewellery crashing on her bed.

In my sound box I would put . . .
The sound of my friends celebrating when they scored a goal,
The sound of the cheers when pupils walk out of school,
The sound of my best friend crying because he grazed his knee,
The sound of the dinnerladies threatening to put you in detention.

In my soundbox I would put . . .
The sound of my boiled egg bubbling in the pan,
The sound of my sister screaming for a drink,
The sound of my dad laughing at the TV
The sound of my mum shouting at the bin men.

In my soundbox I would put . . .
The sound of the pain coming from the injured footballer,
The sound of the crowd singing 'We are the champions'
The sound of the players clapping when they've won the match
And the sound of the fans who lost, driving home in anger.

Daniel Turner (9)
Woodside Junior School

The Crescent Moon

The moon is a spoiler from a fast car
The moon is a piece of Terry's Chocolate Orange
The moon is a smiley face
The moon is a banana that is about to get eaten
The moon is a slice of lemon floating in a drink
The moon is a big boomerang flying in the air
The moon is an overgrown toenail.

Lewis Slane (9)
Woodside Junior School

The Crescent Moon

The moon is like a football hanging in the sky.
The moon is like a crystal shining clear and bright.
The moon is like a lantern shining in the sky
with stars like insects buzzing by.
The moon is like a face looking down on Woodside School.
The moon is like a banana waiting to be eaten.

Lewis Hill (9)
Woodside Junior School

My Fireworks Poem

Whoosh! Pop! Bang!
Red, orange, white,
Sparkle, sparkle, sparkle
In the velvet
Night!

Coral Jardine (9)
Woodside Junior School

THE MOON

The moon is a
sideways face
winking back at me.

The moon is a
dinosaur's tail
wiggling about.

The moon is a
slice of lemon
floating about in a drink.

The moon is a
bent bit of copper
just brown and rusty.

The moon is a
target
waiting to be aimed.

The moon is a
golden bit of cheese
just waiting to be eaten.

Jordan Long (9)
Woodside Junior School

THE OLD MAN GLUM

There was an old man of Glum
Who had a very big tum
And a big bum
And liked to chew gum
That happy old man of Glum.

Dean Leggatt (9)
Woodside Junior School

Apostrophe Poem

Best remembered:
My kitten's fur
My mum's cooking,
My dad's laughing,
My dad's games,
My mum's cuddles,
My friend's tickles,
My brother's help.

Best forgotten:
My kitten's bite,
My mum's shouts,
My dad's smacks,
My mum's cooking (sometimes),
My friend's scratches,
My brother's nightmares.

Charlie McCormick (8)
Woodside Junior School

The Crescent Moon

The moon is like a lemon in a glass of Coke
The moon is like a banana just about to be eaten
The moon is like a Terry's Chocolate Orange
The moon is like a Siki symbol
The moon is like a boomerang
The moon is like a slice of orange
The moon is like a floating boat
The moon is like a mouth looking down at me.

Lindsey Gwilliam (9)
Woodside Junior School

MOON

The moon is like a banana
shaped like a nose
as big as a toenail
like a fingernail.
I like lemon
shaped like the moon
sitting on a plate
like a sideways face.

The moon is like a lemon
floating in a drink
it's like a Terry's Chocolate Segment
like a moon.

Joe Couzens (9)
Woodside Junior School

APOSTROPHE POEM

Best remembered:
My dog's small size
My goldfish's largeness
My bike's stunts
My mum's brilliance.

Best forgotten:
My brother's laziness
My dad's smelly feet
My mum's leaving me with my sister
My sister's moaning
My cousin falling over.

Jamie Mills (9)
Woodside Junior School

The Sound Box

(Based on 'Magic Box' by Kit Wright)

In my sound box I will put . . .
I will put some children shouting from purple class
I will put the sound of the radio going *bleep, bleep, bleep.*
The roar of a lion in the African jungle.
The cry of a newborn baby.

The laugh of my sister, from my bedroom.
The thunder and lightning, coming from outside.
The sound of people shouting in the playground.

The cry of children coming from the playground
The quiet talking, from the Class 5R.
The ghostly sound, coming from the room next door
The werewolf sound, coming from the house next door.

Melissa Theedom (9)
Woodside Junior School

My Country

If I had a country of my own
I would make all wars stop
If I had a country of my own
It would always be hot.

If I had a country of my own
I would be the ruler
If I had a country of my own
Everyone would do the hula.

If I had a country of my own
All the birds would be singing
If I had a country of my own
I would always be swimming.

Rebecca Vernon (10)
Woodside Junior School

THE MOON

The moon is like . . .
a boomerang frozen in the sky
a smile turned sideways,
and like a slice of Terry's Chocolate Orange.

The moon is like . . .
a toenail bitten off and put on the sky,
a slice of hair dyed white
and a banana gone old.

The moon is like . . .
a slice of lemon on cola
a tap which you can pull up and down
and a lion's tooth so sharp.

The moon is like . . .
a nail which is bent
a ruler melted and bent
and a lake frozen sideways.

Keith Wheeler (9)
Woodside Junior School

EVERYDAY SOUNDS

The sound of cars is like an engine running
The sound of people talking is like a rumble across the classroom
The sound of pencils writing is like a soft scraping sound
The sound of a train running along the track is like a drum beating.
The sound of pages being turned in a book is like a light ripping sound.
The sound of the wind is like a soft whistling sound.
The sound of aeroplanes taking off is like a loud crashing sound.

Bethany Scott (10)
Woodside Junior School

THE SOUND BOX

(Based on 'Magic Box' by Kit Wright)

In my magical sound box you can hear . . .
The lightning crashing against the window,
And the baby crying,
While the parents are rowing.

In my magical sound box you can hear . . .
The monkeys swing tree to tree,
You can hear children shouting
When they are playing.

In my magical sound box you can hear . . .
The windows crashing,
You can hear boys shouting
As they run with fear.

Paris Hanson (9)
Woodside Junior School

THE MOON

The moon looks like a croissant
cooking in the oven.

The moon looks like a cheesy Wotsit
although it is not orange.

The moon looks like a toenail
chopped from a foot.

The moon looks like a fraction of Terry's Chocolate Orange
moving down my throat.

The moon looks like a grain of rice
burning on my tongue.

Harry Forrester (9)
Woodside Junior School

Sand Box

(Based on 'Magic Box' by Kit Wright)

In my sand box I see a . . .
Massive sand monster trying to eat me.
A sand dragon breathing sandy fire.
Argh! They've killed me.
Let me start again yeh, yeh.

In my sand box I see a . . .
Pile of quicksand *slurp, slurp,* argh
A sand dinosaur trying to stamp on me
Argh! They've killed me
Let me start again, yeh, yeh.

In my sand box I see an . . .
Army of sand shooting sand bullets at me
A sand man throwing sand balls
Argh! They've killed me
Let's not start again because
I'm bored. Yeh, yeh!

Charlotte Cross (10)
Woodside Junior School

The Sound Box

(Based on 'Magic Box' by Kit Wright)

In my sound box I hear a boy shouting at his sister.
I can hear a baby crying for a bottle.
I can hear cars speeding on the road.
I can hear the police cars bells.
I can hear the schoolboys shouting and screaming.
I can hear a bully fighting the police.
I can hear the cheetahs eating.

Ashley Monckton (9)
Woodside Junior School

TEACHERS

Let me tell you about my school
It's fun to go there, the teachers are cool,
It's called Woodside and Croydon's near
Mrs Johnston is the Deputy and the Head is Mr Wier.

Mr Jenkins is Australian and very tall
He stands like a giant in the hall,
His favourite food is Pot Noodles
He has been seen in assembly drawing doodles.

Mrs Thomas had a different name
We are not quite sure who she became,
Last but not least is blonde Mrs Moore
She could teach you a music score.

So there's my teachers now you know
Teaching us to learn and grow,
Thank you for the help you gave
In my brain I hope to save.

Rianna Matthews (10)
Woodside Junior School

THE CRESCENT MOON

The moon is like a banana
that's floating and glowing in the sky
it is like a big banana just waiting to be eaten.

The moon is like a lemon floating in a drink
the moon is like a lemon just waiting to be sour.

The moon is like a fingernail just waiting to be clipped
the moon is like a fingernail that is really long and sharp.

Christopher Stobbs (10)
Woodside Junior School

The Sound Box

(Based on 'Magic Box' by Kit Wright)

In my sound box
I can hear cars
that beep, beep
and beep.

In my sound box
I can hear babies cry
for their mummies.

In my sound box
I can hear a monkey
that is swinging
through the trees.

In my sound box
I can hear a police car siren.

Daniel O'Connor (10)
Woodside Junior School

You're Like . . .

You're like a lion with strong arms,
You're like a cheetah running through forest,
You smell just like a pig sty, rolling round and round.

You're as ugly as an elephant jumping up and down,
Your legs wobble like a jellyfish on the beach.

Your face looks like a hairy bear eating in the woods,
Your hair is like a furry ball, rolling round and round.

Frances Thompson (10)
Woodside Junior School